Christian
Academic
Writing

Christian Academic Writing

TWELVE PRACTICES AND PRINCIPLES FOR BECOMING A SUCCESSFUL WRITER

Benjamin L. Merkle and
Adrianne Cheek Miles

Baker Academic
a division of Baker Publishing Group
Grand Rapids, Michigan

Published by Baker Academic
a division of Baker Publishing Group
Grand Rapids, Michigan
www.bakeracademic.com

Printed in the United States of America

Library of Congress Cataloging-in-Publication Data
Names: Merkle, Benjamin L., 1971– author. | Miles, Adrianne Cheek, author.
Title: Christian academic writing : twelve practices and principles for becoming a
    successful writer / Benjamin L. Merkle and Adrianne Cheek Miles.
Description: Grand Rapids, Michigan : Baker Academic, a division of Baker Publishing
    Group, 2024. | Includes bibliographical references and index.
Identifiers: LCCN 2023023290 | ISBN 9781540965998 (paperback) | ISBN
    9781540967305 (casebound) | ISBN 9781493444465 (ebook) | ISBN 9781493444472
    (pdf)
Subjects: LCSH: Christian literature—Authorship. | Academic writing.
Classification: LCC BR44 .M47 2024 | DDC 808.06/623—dc23/eng/20230717
LC record available at https://lccn.loc.gov/2023023290

24   25   26   27   28   29   30   7   6   5   4   3   2   1

Contents

Preface

BENJAMIN L. MERKLE

WHY WRITE ABOUT WRITING?

I never set out to pen a book on academic writing. The idea of it wasn't in the back of my mind just waiting for the right time and the right context. It wasn't even on my radar. But it emerged one day when a colleague approached and asked me, "How do you do it?" I replied, "Do what?" He said, "How do you write so much?" This was not a question I was expecting, and I had no profound answer to offer. I didn't think much about it until it happened again a few days later on a different campus. A fellow professor questioned me, "How do you write so much?" Again, I was dumbstruck. I thought to myself, "I don't know. I go to my office every day, teach some classes, answer emails, meet with students, and, if I have time, I write."

Clearly some of my colleagues were looking for tips because they noticed that I was able to crank out a steady stream of articles and books. But what was it that allowed me to produce more books than others? Did I have a secret method? If so, I wasn't aware of it. As I went to my hotel room that night I became disappointed in myself for not being able to offer a thoughtful response to what made me successful in writing and publishing books. Certainly, I was doing something that I could share with others. So that night I began to make a list of practices and principles that enabled me to write and publish. In the end, I came up with twelve. Although most of these insights are not original to me, they came from my own personal experience. I then wrote a paragraph or two explaining the gist of each one.

After several weeks, I came back to the outline and decided to take the next step: I would write an essay entitled "How to Write with a View toward Publishing." I began expanding each of the twelve points. I also bought and read about thirty of the best books on writing to support and validate my insights. After several more weeks I had produced a ten-thousand-word essay. At this point, I thought I was done with the topic. I shared my insights at several conferences and was ready to move on to something else. Several people, however, urged me to turn my essay into a book. But I felt that I had said what I needed to say, and I wasn't sure I had the motivation to significantly expand the material (from ten thousand to fifty thousand words). Perhaps you have read an entire book that you thought could have been reduced to a single chapter. I didn't want to write such a work. So I thought if I was going to expand this material into a book, the project would greatly benefit from having a coauthor.

This was when Dr. Adrianne Miles came into the picture. She teaches at the same school where I work (and that makes coauthoring somewhat easier). She is brilliant, she holds a PhD in linguistics, and she teaches literature and courses related to writing and publishing (the precise topic of this book). So a few years ago I asked her if she would be interested in coauthoring this book. Thankfully, she said yes. So, how did we divvy up the work? Very simply—she took my initial ten-thousand-word essay and expanded it with new contexts, fuller explanations, and helpful illustrations, and she added a practical section at the end of every chapter ("The Next Level").

This book began as my idea and is based on my experiences and my initial reflections, yet in the end Adrianne has written the majority of the text by adding her thoughtful expansions to my all-too-brief essay. This is a truly collaborative work.

WHY THIS BOOK?

The previous section focused on why this book was written and the context that led us to begin writing it. But why did we write a book on *academic* writing? I am not an English teacher (though Adrianne is). I have no degrees in literature or writing or English. But I do have writing and publishing experience.

Credibility is important. When you need surgery or a root canal or physical therapy, you want to find a credible surgeon, endodontist, or therapist. When I was considering shoulder surgery, I didn't simply google "orthopedic surgeon" and then make an appointment ("Just OK is not OK"). I asked around to find the best surgeon in the area, one who had a proven track record. And if you want advice for writing with a view toward publishing, you want someone with a credible reputation. So let me explain to you why I am qualified to write this book. Like Paul, who reluctantly shared the litany of his sufferings in 2 Corinthians 11, I reluctantly offer you my credentials.

I have published books with seven different publishing companies (Baker, Zondervan, B&H, Crossway, Kregel, Lexham, and Peter Lang). I have authored nine books, coauthored eight, and edited more than thirty. I have published more than twenty academic articles in about a dozen different journals. I am also the series editor for the 40 Questions Series (Kregel), the series editor for a twenty-volume series called Planted in the Word, which provides forty days of guided study through each New Testament book (Lexham/Kirkdale), the editor of *Southeastern Theological Review* (since 2015), and the New Testament editor for the *Grace and Truth Study Bible* with HarperCollins. Along the way I have worked with more than a hundred different authors or potential authors. Again, to reference Paul, "I have been a fool! You forced me to it" (2 Cor. 12:11).

This book is not a manual for research, writing, and publishing. It is not a step-by-step guide to walk you through those processes.[1] Rather, this book is full of practical and proven advice to help you with your writing projects. I hope this book becomes the fresh breeze that puts wind in your sails, helping you to cross the finish line (i.e., turn in a writing assignment; complete a project, thesis, or dissertation; or publish an article or book).

Special thanks to Bryan Dyer, who believed this was a worthy project, and to Anna English, Eric Salo, and the team at Baker Academic

---

1. For such a book, I recommend Nijay K. Gupta, *The Writer: A Guide to Research, Writing, and Publishing in Biblical Studies* (Eugene, OR: Cascade Books, 2022).

who guided us through the process. We also thank Faith Haberer and Alex Carr for their willingness to proofread the manuscript as well as offer helpful suggestions. And we would be remiss if we didn't thank the administration and faculty at Southeastern Baptist Theological Seminary. Finally, we thank our families, who helped us redeem time for writing by picking up chores we let slide and patiently waiting five more minutes to eat dinner on more than one occasion. Writing does not happen in a vacuum, and we are grateful for the opportunity we have to instruct and inspire.

1

Love Your Topics

A book on writing ought to start at the beginning of the writing process. Academic writing doesn't begin with paper and pen or by opening a word-processing program on your computer. Writing starts with an interest that becomes a passion. Passion is one of the most important ingredients in academic writing, but it is not the only necessary ingredient. As we will discuss in this chapter, passion coupled with discipline produces writing.

PASSION OR LOVE

We begin with passion because, for most of us, writing is hard work. It takes a lot of time and energy. "If you find that writing is hard," notes William Zinsser, "it's because it is hard."[1] In order for us to be motivated and persevere in writing, we must really care about the topics we study, research, and write on. Consider the things or people about which you are passionate. The first things that spring to your mind may not be academic. In fact, they likely are not. You may think about the special someone in your life, a favorite sports team, or a

1. William Zinsser, *On Writing Well: The Classic Guide to Writing Nonfiction*, 7th ed., rev. and updated (New York: Harper Perennial, 2006), 9.

1

hobby. I (Adrianne) would think of my family, baking, or vacation planning. I am passionate about those things. For example, when I am planning a vacation, I spend hours researching the destination. I read about it, talk about it, and even write about it—if you count emails and texts as writing. I once actually made guide booklets for a trip to Mexico with extended family members. I may have taken that one too far, but I was so passionate about our trip and so excited about the research I was doing that I had to "publish" my findings.

Not many academic writing books address the importance of loving your topic, but how will you be able to spend dozens, even hundreds, of hours on a topic that doesn't fill you with passion? Before anyone gets hung up on the idea of love and passion in the academic world, we need to demystify the idea. Our relationships with academic topics can be, but are not necessarily, monogamous. In other words, you can feel passionate about more than one academic topic in your lifetime and more than one topic at the same time. Writer and editor Andrew Le Peau says writers should "pay attention to what gives [them] joy and energy."[2] Think about the academic topics that give you joy or that energize you. What do you find yourself thinking about in the shower, on your commute, or when you're cutting the grass or exercising? You might mull over a concept that intrigues you, a theory or principle that you question, or even some point or analysis that really annoys you. Academics can be passionate about topics that they find irksome. Passion for a topic motivates a scholar to enter the broader conversation about that topic.

Although few romance novels chronicle a person falling in love with scholarly subject matter, academics tend to fall in love with topics in ways that resemble popular romantic love tropes: love at first sight, friends to lovers, enemies to lovers. Don't put undue pressure on yourself to have a "love at first sight" experience with an academic topic. Recognize that fondness can lead to passion as can initial repulsion. Be aware of the topics and concepts you find yourself

---

2. Andrew T. Le Peau, *Write Better: A Lifelong Editor on Craft, Art, and Spirituality* (Downers Grove, IL: InterVarsity, 2019), 173. Similarly, Nijay K. Gupta says, "Your writing, in most cases, should be inspired by your passions, those subjects that are meaningful to you." *The Writer: A Guide to Research, Writing, and Publishing in Biblical Studies* (Eugene, OR: Cascade Books, 2022), 94.

lingering over, either with positive or negative thoughts. You may be at the beginning of what could become a beautiful relationship.

I (Adrianne) asked a friend of mine who recently finished her dissertation how she fell in love with her topic. I knew she was passionate about it because when she talked about it, she always talked fast, as if she had too much to say and too little time to get it all out. She surprised me by telling me that she began with something that bothered her—the seeming divide between academic theological studies and the life of the local church. Through her research, she sought to answer this question: What is the relationship between theology and the church? She had discovered the writings of T. F. Torrance, and she told me, "Honestly, the desire for clarity to think with Torrance to better understand the gospel and theology from within the context of God reconciling the world to himself in Christ was the primary motivator to push me through the writing process."[3] She explained that "being forced to do focused and detailed reflection, in time, grew [her] affections for [Christ] even more, and led [her] to awe and wonder at the gospel."[4] I would argue that any Christian writer who loves his or her topic is positioned to gain a better understanding of the God we serve—a God of details, order, and compassion for his creation.

People write about academic topics that energize them and bring them joy. These are also the reasons we are writing this book. We have a passion to help Christian academics (students and faculty) find their voices and participate in scholarly conversations. We know that students and other academics have intriguing and important things to say, but often they refrain from academic writing because of various insecurities. (We discuss some of these insecurities specifically in chapter 4.) Over the years, we have noticed that a little bit of encouragement can go a long way in helping academics find the courage to write. Successful writers can often point to an influential person in their lives who encouraged them in their craft. For example, Stephen King's mother challenged him to make up his own story. He did, and when his mother read it, "she said it was good enough

---

3. Christy Thornton, interviewed by Adrianne Miles, Wake Forest, NC, October 28, 2021.
4. Thornton, interview.

to be in a book. Nothing anyone has said to [him] since has made [him] feel any happier."[5] As professors, we realize that we have some influence over students and colleagues, and we want to use that influence to encourage others (to encourage you) to engage in academic conversations through writing. I (Adrianne) had the opportunity to edit a workbook for a women's leadership conference at my institution. The coordinator of this conference had invited various students, graduates, and professionals to contribute chapters. One of the contributors had been in my British literature class a few years earlier. I had commended her research and writing and tried (unsuccessfully) to persuade her to change her major to English. When I read her chapter for the workbook, I was blown away, and I told her so. She responded: "This made my day!!!!! Like really! Thank you for your encouragement!"[6] Her reaction energized me and filled me with joy. Opportunities like this motivated us to write this book.

Perhaps a more basic passion motivating this book is that both of us love writing. But let us clarify. We don't love writing in the way we love a vacation on the coast. As we have already acknowledged, writing is hard work. But we love writing about our research interests because we love discussing our topics. We want to share and gain information—to move the scholarly conversations along—through writing. At the same time, there are elements of the writing craft that we really do like. It is a joy to find the best word or phrase to express an idea, to craft a sentence so beautiful that it is almost poetry, to create transition sentences that neatly unify two ideas, and this joy motivates us to continuously strive to improve our writing.

WRITING IS HARD WORK

Regardless of how passionate any of us are about our research and writing focus, writing is hard work. It's the passion that keeps us going. While I (Adrianne) enjoyed planning that trip to Mexico and writing that guide booklet, it was work. There were long hours, late nights, and frustrations—and that was just for a vacation. The long

---

5. Stephen King, *On Writing: A Memoir of the Craft* (New York: Scribner, 2000), 29.
6. Kathryn Zorn, email message to Adrianne Miles, January 14, 2022.

hours and frustrations increase exponentially when I'm working on an academic paper. The last paper I submitted to an academic journal began with a first draft of the research, continued with drafts of presentations at two conferences, and was followed by several additional drafts to hone and polish my work. The total editing time spent on those documents comes to 850 hours. That's equivalent to thirty-five days working around the clock! And this figure does not include the time I spent reading and researching, although some of that was done with drafts opened on my computer. Why would anyone spend so much time on a project? Why did I put this level of work into that article? I did it because I loved my topic. I'm passionate about dialects. I believe language varieties contribute to identity and perception, and I am fascinated by the way dialogue affects characterization in fiction. Because I love the interaction of language and culture, I could spend the rest of this chapter talking about it. I won't because that is not the point of this chapter. My point here is to help us recognize and accept that writing is hard work.

Writing is *hard* work because it is often *long* work. Helen Sword calculates that her "published research output averaged out to only about one hundred words per hour."[7] Published or submitted writing (for a class, to fulfill graduate school requirements, or for potential publication) comes to be through hours of research and drafting in addition to the hours of discussions with instructors and colleagues. We often work through setbacks, false starts, restarts, research struggles, time management struggles, and negative feedback. Such things can end up making our work stronger, but they all take time. We can't fast-forward a writing project. When a reader picks up a paper, article, chapter, or book at the library, she may quickly move from one page to the next or skip to the end like a time traveler. But unlike Doctor Who, the writer has no access to a time machine and instead is the "weary traveler, [who] must always take the slower path."[8] There are no shortcuts in good writing, so we had better love

7. Helen Sword, *Air & Light & Time & Space: How Successful Academics Write* (Cambridge, MA: Harvard University Press, 2017), 12.

8. *Doctor Who*, series 2, episode 4, "The Girl in the Fireplace," directed by Euros Lyn, written by Steven Moffat, featuring David Tennant, Billie Piper, and Sophia Myles, aired May 6, 2006, on BBC.

our topics. Our passion and enthusiasm must sustain us through hundreds of hours of work—hard work.

WRITING IS NOT ABOUT MONEY—IT'S ABOUT SHARING

Besides being difficult, academic writing is not particularly lucrative. There is little money to be made by publishing. Most journals don't pay anything. We currently know of only two academic journals that offer a small stipend for a published essay. Most publishers pay book royalties twice a year (though some pay quarterly), and most academic books sell only a few thousand copies during their life span. When it comes to publishing dissertations, only a few hundred copies are usually sold (mostly to libraries), and sometimes the publisher will require the author to make a one-time payment to help defray costs. Yes, you heard us correctly: it sometimes costs money to have a book published. We've heard stories of authors who received royalty checks of less than $100 after a full year of sales. Publishers usually offer authors 12–15 percent from the sales of the book as royalties. This amount, however, is derived from the wholesale price (i.e., the price the publisher sells the book for and not the retail price). So, if a book retails at $30, it will usually sell at wholesale for $15, so the author will receive $1.80–$2.25 for every book sold. If an author sells a thousand books a year, they will receive two checks of $900.00–$1,125.00 (or $1,800.00–$2,250.00 for the year).

Academic writers are not motivated by money. Instead, our enthusiasm about our topics drives us to share what we have learned. We don't write to file our thoughts away, never to be read. We write because we think we have something worth saying. There is a larger scholarly conversation going on, and we believe we can contribute to it in some way. We want to move the collective understanding of a particular aspect of our field one step further along the path. The article that I (Adrianne) worked on for over 850 hours, and for which I received no publication pay, added to the larger ongoing conversation concerning the ways in which social class is communicated in fiction. Social class may be denoted, or marked, in various ways, and much had already been said about fiction writers using locative markers (e.g., characters from lower classes must use the back door whereas those from higher classes use the front door at a non-lower-class home) and physical markers (e.g., lower classes are unkempt, but higher classes are presented as neatly dressed) to characterize individuals. The scholarly conversation already included some work about how fiction writers use dialogue to distinguish between classes. Much more work had been published outside of the fiction-writing conversation about dialects and class in various communities around the world. I felt I could contribute to the conversation about class markers in fiction through an analysis that included locative, physical, and linguistic markers. In my excitement over this topic, I wanted to share it with others and move the larger conversation along.

It may feel daunting at first to share your work with others, so start small. Talk about your research with a colleague or peer. If you are a student, talk with an instructor who works in your field of interest. We will discuss sharing your work more in chapters 8, 9, and 10, but consider presenting your research at a conference. Colleagues and conferences offer great ways to enter the scholarly conversation. Contributing to this conversation motivates academic writers. Let it motivate you, and don't be ashamed to let other people read what you write. Your work moves the conversation forward.

DISCIPLINE

While our passion for our topics and our desire to contribute to the larger conversations are important parts of the writing equation, another crucial element is discipline. Bernard Malamud explains, "How one works, assuming he's disciplined, doesn't matter. If he or she is not disciplined, no sympathetic magic will help."[9] Passion is good. Discipline is good. But disciplined passion is even better. Pursue writing with passion, but also pursue it with discipline. That is when the magic begins.

We will discuss discipline in more detail in chapter 6, but it is important to understand from the outset that no amount of enthusiasm for your topic will produce writing apart from discipline. Like faith without works, writing without discipline is dead. Some writers find

9. Mason Currey, *Daily Rituals: How Artists Work* (New York: Knopf, 2013), 234.

it crucial to write every day. Once we get out of the rhythm of writing, it becomes harder to reengage. Helen Sword reminds us of the many benefits of daily writing:[10]

1. *Daily writing prevents procrastination and blocking:* if you have a scheduled time to write, then when that time comes, you start writing.
2. *Daily writing demystifies the writing process:* those who write every day have no fear of a blank page since they conquer such pages daily by filling them with words.
3. *Daily writing keeps your research always at the top of your mind:* regardless of your busy schedule of meetings, administrative tasks, or teaching, at least some part of the day is spent focused on your research.
4. *Daily writing generates new ideas:* thinking and writing about a topic prompts new modes of thought.
5. *Daily writing adds up incrementally:* three hundred words a day adds up to six thousand by the end of the month—a new chapter or article!
6. *Daily writing helps you figure out what you want to say:* sometimes we don't know what we are going to say until we start saying and forming our arguments on paper.

One thing is certain: if we want to write, then we need to make time in our schedules to do so. Because writing is difficult for most of us, we sometimes have to force ourselves to write when we don't feel like it. We all have friends who are runners. They can call themselves "runners" not only because they like to run but also because they plan to run and then actually run. They run when they are tired, when they don't feel like it, when it is cold out, or when they would rather be doing something else. If we want to call ourselves writers, we need to plan to write.

In the end, however, it doesn't matter how we get there. What matters is that we *do* get there. Sword reminds us that not everyone who is a successful or productive writer gets there the same way. She states:

10. Sword, *Air & Light & Time & Space*, 18.

Some successful academics write daily, others sporadically; some at home, others at work; some on trains or airplanes or during children's sports practice, others in distraction-free environments; some on a word processor, others in longhand or using voice-recognition software; some whenever they have a few minutes free, others only when they have cleared hours or days of uninterrupted time. Some map out a detailed topic outline before they start writing; others write to discover what they have to say.[11]

Ultimately, we need discipline in order to sit down (or stand) and begin writing. Passion or love of a topic is good. Discipline is good. But a disciplined passion is best since it takes the love that we have and helps us faithfully and consistently make it to the finish line of our project.

CONCLUSION

The reason we spend countless hours in the library, in our offices, at the kitchen table—wherever—researching and writing is that we have a deep passion for the topic at hand.[12] If we are writing merely for a promotion, to impress our peers, or for pay, it will not be sustainable.[13] We do what we do because we love truth and beauty.[14] We do what we do because it is a worthwhile pursuit in God's amazing and complex world. My (Ben's) good friend Robert Plummer says, "If something is worth writing, it's worth writing well. If it's worth writing well, it's worth sharing with others." Whether fully justified or not, we academic writers are convinced that what we do is important and matters—and that is what motivates us.

11. Sword, *Air & Light & Time & Space*, 15.
12. Even Zinsser adds, "If you follow your affections you will write well and will engage your readers." *On Writing Well*, 91.
13. In answer to the question, "Do you do it for the money?," Stephen King stated, "The answer is no. Don't now and never did. Yes, I've made a great deal of dough from my fiction, but I never set a single word down on paper with the thought of being paid for it. . . . I have written because it fulfilled me. . . . I did it for the pure joy of the thing. And if you can do it for joy, you can do it forever." *On Writing*, 249.
14. Helen Sword states that "the road to productivity will be a long and tedious one unless you can find meaningful ways to pave it with pleasure." *Air & Light & Time & Space*, 166.

THE NEXT LEVEL

1. In your corner of the academic world, what are you passionate about? What topic do you find yourself talking to your colleagues, friends, or family members about?

   _____

   _____

   _____

2. Count the cost. What is the hardest part of writing for you (e.g., research, a blank screen, organizing your thoughts)?

   _____

   _____

   _____

3. Have you written a paper for a class, conference, or journal that focuses on the topic you listed in question 1 above? Why or why not?

   _____

   _____

   _____

   a. If you have not, it's time to get started. Have a conversation about your interests with someone working in that field.
   b. If you have written a class paper or a conference talk, have a conversation with an instructor or colleague about transforming that work into an article to submit for publication.

2

Keep Reading Material
with You

Most people who write academic works either are full-time students or have full-time jobs that don't primarily or directly involve writing. In fact, we only know one person who makes a living writing, and she writes fiction. Consequently, we must take advantage of any time available to us. One of the strategies we use to maximize our free time is to always have reading material with us.

You may be wondering why we dedicate an entire chapter to reading when this book is about writing. Very few books on writing discuss the importance of reading, but reading is of utmost importance when it comes to writing. As Melissa Donovan discusses in her book on writing fiction, "Without each other, reading and writing cannot exist. They rely on one another. They are two parts of a greater whole."[1] In other words, the more you read, the better you can write. Reading not only increases our knowledge; it also helps us enter the scholarly conversation. Additionally, reading good texts can passively help us with our grammar and vocabulary skills.[2] Writing requires reading.

1. Melissa Donovan, *10 Core Practices for Better Writing* (San Francisco: Swan Hatch, 2013), 7.
2. Donovan, *10 Core Practices*, 8.

WHAT TO READ

Of course, we should be reading materials related to our research topic. Research reading informs us of the work already done in the field. It tells us where the conversation has gone and gives us a clearer understanding of how our own research may move it along. Such reading can also help us formulate questions and hypotheses to further our research as it helps us solidify our understanding of a topic and our perspectives concerning controversies in our field. This kind of reading is foundational to academic writing. One must know what has already been said before one can know if she has something worthwhile to say. While research material likely makes up the bulk of what an academic writer reads, it should not be the only kind of reading in her life.

Academic writers should be reading the kinds of books they would like to submit as manuscripts; they should be reading articles in the journals in which they would like to be published. This we will call genre reading. If you want to write a monograph on the life and literary contributions of Anne Locke, you should read similar monographs written about other authors. Are those other monographs organized chronologically according to the life of the subject, topically according to the literary contributions, or in some other way? Which do you prefer? Which is easier to process as a reader? If there are other monographs that focus on Anne Locke, you will read those as part of your research reading, but you should also do some genre reading to help you understand the style of writing that gets published in that genre. Similarly, if you want to submit an article for publication in *The Journal of Theological Studies* or *Christianity Today*, read some recent issues to give yourself an idea of the style and quality of the articles they publish. These two periodicals, for example, have different audiences with different expectations. Thus, one requires a different writing style from the other. Writing instructors often remind their students to "know your audience." Getting to know your audience includes genre reading.

In addition to research and genre reading, you should also add books on writing to your reading inventory. Unless your advanced degree is in writing, it has probably been a while since you've been in a writing class. Books on writing can help us remember things we once knew that have since been buried under more pressing matters. They also teach us things we may have never learned before. For example, despite my undergraduate degree in English, I (Adrianne) never learned that "the adverb is not your friend."[3] Adverbs are words that should be used *sparingly*, if at all, in professional writing.[4] *Interestingly*, editors slashed "interestingly" from my manuscripts. If only I had read Roy Peter Clark first, I would have known better. I would have understood that I should not tell my readers that something is interesting; rather, I should show them that it is interesting in how I write about it. There are several great books on writing style, and we recommend the following ones:

Clark, Roy Peter. *Writing Tools: 55 Essential Strategies for Every Writer*. New York: Little, Brown, 2016. In addition to points of style, Clark helps writers work from a plan as he encourages us to keep our readers at the forefront of our minds. He offers useful writing habits among his fifty-five tools as well.

LaRocque, Paula. *The Book on Writing: The Ultimate Guide to Writing Well*. Arlington, TX: Grey & Guvnor, 2003. Although LaRocque's book is directed to fiction writers, her first and final sections, which focus on writing mechanics, are helpful for various types of writers. Many of her points in the section on storytelling devices can (and should) be adapted to academic writing. For example, academic writers should recognize the speedbumps in their manuscripts and use them to their advantage. LaRocque defines speedbumps as "little hurdles that impede flow because they stop the reader, if only for a moment" (181). Grammar mistakes, excessively long sentences, complicated phrasing, and using the wrong word are a few examples of speedbumps for readers.

Strunk, William, Jr., and E. B. White. *The Elements of Style*. 4th edition. Boston: Pearson, 2000. This book is a classic, and at

3. Stephen King, *On Writing: A Memoir of the Craft* (New York: Scribner, 2000), 124.

4. See, e.g., Roy Peter Clark, *Writing Tools: 55 Essential Strategies for Every Writer* (New York: Little, Brown, 2016), 27–30.

eighty-five pages, it is accessible even to the busiest academics. There are other editions with Strunk alone or other coauthors. You should be able to get your hands on any one of these editions for less than ten dollars, some less than five dollars. This book is a must for your craft toolbox. You'll find yourself going back to it again and again.

Zinsser, William. *On Writing Well: The Classic Guide to Writing Nonfiction.* 7th edition. Revised and updated. New York: Harper Perennial, 2006. Zinsser divides his book into four main parts: "Principles," "Methods," "Forms," and "Attitudes." In "Principles," he focuses on style at the sentence level. "Methods" continues his discussion of style but at the paragraph and whole-text level. In "Forms," he discusses different types of nonfiction writing. He concludes with "Attitudes," wherein he touches on some of the struggles common to writing.

But don't stop with books that help you improve your style and sentence structure. You must also read books specifically written to help academic writers. You're off to a great start reading this book! These books help readers understand and overcome the unique challenges of academic writing. Many books on writing tend to focus on fiction, and while they can be encouraging and even inspiring, much of the information in them simply does not apply in the academic world. Academic writers must understand the larger genre of academic writing. They often feel pressure to "publish or perish," while carrying heavy course loads, serving on various committees, and advising handfuls of students (or more). Books that focus specifically on academic writing address such concerns and offer hope and help. We have benefited from the following academic writing books:

Goodson, Patricia. *Becoming an Academic Writer: 50 Exercises for Paced, Productive, and Powerful Writing.* 2nd edition. Thousand Oaks, CA: Sage, 2017. This book is helpful because it walks readers through exercises in writing. How do you become a better writer? You write. Goodson begins by discussing the effect of writing habits in the first hundred pages. The last hundred pages are writing exercises along with examples that are designed to help us stop procrastinating and start writing.

Jensen, Joli. *Write No Matter What: Advice for Academics*. Chicago: University of Chicago Press, 2017. Jensen doesn't discuss writing mechanics as much as she discusses the challenges of academic writing. She works to demystify academic writing and move writers toward a craftsman-like approach to their work. She helps readers think through the time, space, and energy they need to write. She also challenges some writing-related myths, a few of which we discuss in chapter 4. She ends by encouraging academics to foster writing support groups.

Sword, Helen. *Air & Light & Time & Space: How Successful Academics Write*. Cambridge, MA: Harvard University Press, 2017. As does Jensen, Sword encourages writers to carve out the time and space necessary to write. Sword focuses on building various writing habits and reminds us of the positive factors that motivate us to pursue academic writing.

Sword, Helen. *Stylish Academic Writing*. Cambridge, MA: Harvard University Press, 2012. As the title suggests, this book is all about writing style and will help writers learn to hone their craft. From word choices to the structure of the book or article, Sword helps us think carefully not just about *what* we write but about *how* we write.

We cannot overemphasize the importance of reading well if you want to write well. The majority of reading, likely 70–80 percent, will be research reading. The remaining 20–30 percent should be divided between genre reading and the craft of writing. While doing your research, you should have a genre text and a craft text going at the same time. You might put one on your bedside table and read a chapter each morning or keep one on the breakfast table to enjoy in small chunks with your coffee and bagel every day. The important point is not to overlook genre and craft reading when you are in the throes of research reading. Research, genre, and craft reading should not be done sequentially but simultaneously as you research and write.

MAKE READING EASIER

We realize that we have suggested a lot of reading, and we want to help you manage your reading tasks well. You may be reading books, chapters in books, or articles. As the title of this chapter says, keep reading material with you so that you can take advantage of various pockets of time throughout your day. You may have reading materials stacked on your desk, your kitchen table, and your nightstand—and that is great because it means you are reading several things at once. But you also need to have something in your bag at all times. Carrying around several books (which are often quite heavy) is not ideal, however. Most of the time we don't need to read an entire book but only a section or a chapter. Why carry around the whole book when it would suffice to photocopy a few (or many) pages? And since photocopying for personal use does not breach any copyright or fair use guidelines, you've got nothing to lose and much to gain by photocopying reading material.

Why photocopy material? There are several helpful benefits. (Of course, another strategy is to use digital versions of books and articles. If this is your preference, then most of the benefits mentioned below would likewise apply to that method.) First, you can more freely highlight and mark the text. I (Ben) like to highlight significant quotes, material to cite in footnotes, and key insights. Some people are hesitant to highlight or write in books. Photocopying can free the conscience, allowing for more aggressive note-taking in the books or articles they read. Additionally, many books are bulky and difficult to keep open, whereas photocopied versions are more user-friendly and much lighter.

Photocopying your texts makes it easier to keep them with you so that you can read when you find yourself with a little extra time here and there. You should keep at least one photocopied chapter or article with you always. Academics tend to travel with a backpack or satchel. If you have not yet developed that habit and pride yourself on traveling light, consider adding a bag to your accessories, or at least planting a few texts in your car. With reading materials in your bag, you can read whenever you find yourself waiting. I (Adrianne) have gotten a great deal of reading done in carpool lines before the dismissal bell would ring when picking up my children from school.

Dentists' and doctors' offices are also good places to read. Think about the lines you stand in during the week (e.g., ordering food or banking) or the times you wait for something to begin (e.g., a movie, chapel, or a meeting). Some of these wait times may be too short to pull out your chapter and start reading, but other times they drag on and on, and you can be productive by reading while you wait. We will talk more about redeeming time for reading in the next chapter. Our goal in this chapter is to prepare you so that you are ready to redeem that time when it presents itself.

A second reason to photocopy your research reading is that it makes double-checking references and quotes much easier and faster. Having the freedom to mark your photocopied versions is more conducive to verification of accuracy and page numbers of quoted or referenced material. Perhaps we should say a word about the need to double-check source material. Because it is far too easy for errors to creep into our work, it is essential to go back and ensure that we have accurately cited the material. In fact, in my (Adrianne's) most recent journal publication, the journal required me to submit a copy of the title page and the quoted page for each quote in my text. Luckily, I had photocopied most of my sources, but I did have to go back to the library to hunt down a few.

A third reason that photocopying is helpful is that you can keep the material for your paper, chapter, or book together. I (Ben) have file folders of resources used for the material I have written. I keep them together so that if I ever need to go back and reference something, I know precisely where to find it.

Again, the main point is to have reading material with you whenever you might have free time. Keep one or two photocopied texts with you at all times. It is easier for you to read when the material is handy. We also encourage you to put a few other necessities for reading in your bag. You want to be able to underline important points or write questions in the margins, so add a pen, pencil, and highlighter to your bag. If you don't add all three, you'll find yourself wishing you had the one you left out, so put them all in. Also put in a sticky note pad for flagging pages or making notes for future research or cross-references. A final suggestion for your bag may seem less obvious: invest in a small but reliable reading light. I (Adrianne) have been ready to read while waiting for the start of baseball games or band concerts only to find that there is not enough light for me to see the print clearly. I've used my phone flashlight on occasion, but the better option is a clip-on reading light. The one I use now is rechargeable, so I don't have to worry about batteries. It also has three levels of brightness, which I've found to be quite handy.

CONCLUSION

As we stated at the beginning of this chapter, reading is necessary for writing. Stephen King explains, "If you want to be a writer, you must do two things above all others: read a lot and write a lot."[5] Because we want you to be a successful writer, we have given you some tools to maximize your free time for reading. Now that your bag is packed and you are ready to pull out reading materials wherever you find yourself, we will help you in the next chapter to recognize pockets of time that you can redeem for reading.

THE NEXT LEVEL

1. What have you read that positively influenced your writing? How did it affect your writing?

_____

_____

_____

2. Considering the three types of reading discussed in this chapter—research reading, genre reading, and craft reading—what percentage of each are you doing right now?

_____

_____

5. King, *On Writing*, 145.

3. If you have never engaged in genre reading or craft reading, how will you start? Which book or books do you want to purchase or borrow from the library? Make a plan for acquiring these books and then get them.

_____

_____

_____

4. Do you think photocopying (or digitally scanning) texts is helpful? Why or why not?

_____

_____

5. What items do you need in your bag to enable you to read anywhere? (It's OK to add items like a water bottle or chewing gum. Know yourself and what will help you get reading.) Pack your bag now.

_____

_____

_____

3

Redeem Time for Reading and Writing

You may be thinking that your time is stretched too thin already. What time could possibly be redeemed for reading and writing? We submit that there are pockets of time in your life that you may not notice because our culture has trained you not to notice them. Fairly large pockets of time can be found in the evenings and during weekends, but our culture tells us that those are "me times" or family times. We are in no way suggesting that you give up the personal downtime that you need or neglect your family in any way. Instead, we are suggesting that you reconsider the potential of working on your writing projects during some of these times.

We agree with Helen Sword that writing is "any research-related activity that moves the writing project forward."[1] In other words, the different types of reading discussed in chapter 2 are part of the writing process. Some elements of the process take more concentrated attention than others. As you plan your work, consider the times of day when you are more focused and the times you are less focused. Eviatar Zerubavel distinguishes between "A-time" and "B-time," describing

1. Helen Sword, *Air & Light & Time & Space: How Successful Academics Write* (Cambridge, MA: Harvard University Press, 2017), 17.

A time as "those somewhat sacred, 'prime' time slots you choose to reserve for your writing and during which you obviously try to be at your best."[2] B-time is project-related work that we do outside of those prime-time slots. B-time may include reading, revising, or editing. Academics tend to be more aware of A-time than B-time. In chapter 6 we will focus more on A-time, but at this point we want to help you identify and use more of your B-time for your writing projects.

As we've already stated, we have other jobs. We don't get paid to write. We get paid to teach. We spend most of our nine-to-five workdays preparing to teach, teaching, and grading. If we only had forty hours a week in which to read or write, then we would only be able to research and write during school breaks—which might not be a bad thing, depending on your situation in life. But if you think prolific writers who also have other jobs somehow figure out how to pump out scholarly tomes by only working forty-hour weeks, you are gravely mistaken. Although I (Ben) don't keep track, I would guess that I typically work about sixty hours a week. If you have small kids, then this is neither possible nor wise. But if you want to publish, you have to be willing to sacrifice some of your personal or "down" time (notice we do not say family time). If I work sixty hours a week and you work only forty hours a week, then every month I have eighty more hours of productivity than you (equivalent to two extra weeks a month). That is a significant amount of time for research and writing.

REDEEMING EVENINGS AND WEEKENDS

We all have free time in the evenings (which does not mean that we all have the same amount of free time). What do you do with your free time? Many of us, being tired from a day's work, simply don't feel like reading or writing. So we sit and watch TV—catching up on the latest season of our favorite show or sporting event. We can easily justify watching ten hours of television a week. There's nothing wrong with that per se, but we need to realize that we are potentially squandering valuable time that could be used to research, read, or write. There is someone else, a prolific writer, who is using time like

2. Eviatar Zerubavel, *The Clockwork Muse: A Practical Guide to Writing Theses, Dissertations, and Books* (Cambridge, MA: Harvard University Press, 1999), 34.

that to write another journal article or book. I (Ben) sometimes tell my doctoral students that if they have more than one or two shows that they keep up with, then their free time is going to TV and not writing. Since I'm already stepping on toes, allow me to step on some more: if it is important to you to keep up with multiple sports but you still hope to publish regularly, just know that it's probably not going to happen—something has to give.

Joli Jensen suggests that academics should spend a week keeping a "reverse day planner."[3] If we feel that we do not have any extra time in our busy lives, recording how we are actually spending our time can help us recognize overindulgences and redeem time for our writing projects. You will find that you have more time than you thought, but not as much as you wish, to work on your project. Count the hours in your week or semester that you can dedicate to reading and writing. We doubt you'll find another forty hours in your week. But even when pockets of time are not huge, they are valuable, and as such, they must be protected if you want to produce the kind of work you want to produce. It is not enough to find the time, although that is an important first step. We must "identify, count, and then secure [our] writing time each week."[4]

To identify opportunities for reading and writing, we need to think about time differently. We can't make more of it, but we can redeem time for our priorities. We waste a lot of time in the evenings because we claim to be too tired, but really we have trained our minds to shut off so that we can't even read a book after five o'clock. We need to re-examine our B-times for our writing projects. When do you get home from work? When do you go to bed? Can you carve out thirty minutes or an hour to work on a writing project? If you have small children, you might block out some time after they go to bed. It will be challenging at first, especially if you are used to vegging out after the kids are in bed, but you can retrain yourself. When my (Adrianne's) boys were in grade school, I frequently read during their extracurricular activities. Weeknight baseball games were one of my favorite times to read. I could cover dozens of pages during their warm-up time,

3. Joli Jensen, *Write No Matter What: Advice for Academics* (Chicago: University of Chicago Press, 2017), 23.
4. Jensen, *Write No Matter What*, 26.

and even during the particularly slow games. But I would put down my book and pick up my camera when one of my sons was at bat or when he took the field. I also managed to read during basketball game warm-ups. (I never managed to read during a basketball game!) Redeeming reading time was not limited to athletic venues. When I would drop my son off early for a band concert, it was pointless to go back home for thirty minutes. Instead, I would grab a good seat and read until the concert began.

If you are married, ask for your spouse's help to carve out time and retrain yourself. Your spouse may suggest that you work while he or she showers or makes tomorrow's lunches. If your spouse is a reader, he or she may welcome time to read while you are working. My (Adrianne's) husband is an avid sports fan. I enjoy watching some sports with him, but there are other sports that I don't really care about. I can sit on the couch and read while he watches a game. That can be two to three hours of excellent reading time on a weeknight. If you live alone, consider asking a colleague to help you retrain yourself. When I (Adrianne) was working on my dissertation, I worked at a research lab. While lab time was for lab work, a friend and I typically worked later, until six o'clock. That extra hour, from five to six, was "off the clock" and dedicated to dissertation work. You might consider working in your office an hour later—or earlier if you are a morning person—and dedicate that time to your writing project.

Weekends are also great opportunities to redeem time for reading and writing. Again, we are not suggesting that you work during family time or that you spend no time relaxing or visiting with friends. Instead, we are asking you to reexamine your weekends to find pockets of time that you could dedicate to your writing project. If you have teenagers who sleep in on Saturdays, consider rising at your normal time and working until ten in the morning or whenever your teens get up. If you have small children, you could work during their morning or afternoon naps. Stephen King suggests reading while at the laundromat, on the treadmill, and in theater lobbies.[5] Redeeming time can be a challenging habit to cultivate, so start small

5. Stephen King, *On Writing: A Memoir of the Craft* (New York: Scribner, 2000), 104.

until your new habit becomes a lifestyle. You may think that "no one can get a scholarly writing project finished by [reading or] writing only a few minutes every day," but Jensen and many other academic writers, including us, respond that "yes, you can, if that's really all you can manage."[6]

REDEEMING TIME DURING BREAKS AND THE WORKDAY

For those of you who desire to write but are limited to the nine-to-five office hours, let us encourage you to use your breaks and your forty hours a week effectively. We know people who slowly but steadily produce material while writing only during breaks—spring breaks, summer breaks, fall breaks, and winter breaks. Working on writing projects during your breaks does not necessarily mean that you don't get downtime. You may decide to write Monday through Thursday and take Friday off. Or you may decide to write until noon each day and take your afternoons off. To be successful, you must develop a plan and stick to it. We know people who are limited to the nine-to-five workday but block out an hour (or more or less) during every workday to research and write. One friend comes to work an hour early each day. Another dedicates his first hour of work to his projects and doesn't even check email until that hour is up. Some find that four to five in the afternoon is a productive hour with fewer distractions than earlier in the day. The point is to critically evaluate your schedule and find pockets of time that will work for you on a consistent basis, whether that's thirty minutes or two hours. Your other work will get done if you prioritize your writing, but your writing will not get done if you do not prioritize it. To reiterate Jensen, you must secure your writing time.

The key is persistence. Little by little is better than nothing at all. Joyce Carol Oates explains her process: "I write and write and write, and rewrite, and even if I retain only a single page from a full day's work, it *is* a single page, and these pages add up. . . . As a result, I have acquired the reputation over the years of being prolix when in fact I am measured against people who simply don't work as hard

---

6. Jensen, *Write No Matter What*, 20.

or as long. . . . Getting the first draft finished is like pushing a peanut with your nose across a very dirty floor."[7] Many of us can't afford to spend a full day's work on writing. It may be that we can only complete a paragraph in an allotted hour. But if we are persistent, that paragraph will turn into a page, the page into a chapter, and so on.

REDEEMING TIME AND RESTING

Cal Newport advocates a strategy that maintains a strict end point to one's workday—no work after 5:30 p.m. This practice of resting your brain, he asserts, improves the quality of deep work.[8] So are we arguing against what Newport says and what certain studies have shown? Not really. You see, the type of work we do outside the office is almost never deep work. It usually involves reading or work that doesn't involve our full, undivided concentration. Our "after hours" work falls into Zerubavel's "B-time." We do a lot of reading and note-taking during these pockets of time. Even Newport reads after 5:30 p.m. He admits that one of his favorite preplanned leisure activities after his kids have gone to bed is reading interesting books. He summarizes: "If you give your mind something meaningful to do throughout *all* your waking hours, you'll end the day more fulfilled, and begin the next one more relaxed, than if you instead allow your mind to bathe for hours in semi-conscious and unstructured Web surfing. . . . If you want to eliminate the addictive pull of entertainment sites on your time and attention, give your brain a quality alternative."[9] Genre and craft reading, as we discussed in chapter 2, can become your best bedtime reading.

CONCLUSION

In the end, we are not saying something different from what Newport says. Maybe he doesn't call reading *work* and we do. Our point is simply that as scholars, we waste a lot of time in the evenings and on weekends because we have not recognized the pockets of time that

7. Mason Currey, *Daily Rituals: How Artists Work* (New York: Knopf, 2013), 63.
8. Cal Newport, *Deep Work: Rules for Focused Success in a Distracted World* (New York: Grand Central, 2016), 154.
9. Newport, *Deep Work*, 214.

could be secured for reading or writing. We have made television, social media, or video games a priority over our writing projects. As we alluded to at the outset of this chapter, there is nothing wrong with television or any relaxation outlet per se, but there is a point of diminishing returns. Are you more relaxed after three hours of *The Office* than after one hour? If one hour helps you unwind, the next two might be time wasters. If you read just for an hour every weeknight, you will add twenty hours a month of reading time to your writing project. That's eighty hours a semester for reading and note-taking. Imagine how these small changes we have suggested could affect your productivity.

THE NEXT LEVEL

1. Using the reverse day planner Jensen suggests, record all your activity over the next week. (See chart on the following page.) Circle the times you could redeem for reading and writing. Highlight the times you will secure for writing projects.

2. When do you typically get home from work? When do you typically go to bed? What thirty-minute (or one-hour) slot can you carve out to work on a writing project?

3. What are the regular activities in your week that do not need your full attention (e.g., spectating, your child's TV time, waiting for events to begin)?

Time	Monday	Tuesday	Wednesday	Thursday	Friday	Saturday	Sunday
5:00 a.m.							
6:00 a.m.							
7:00 a.m.							
8:00 a.m.							
9:00 a.m.							
10:00 a.m.							
11:00 a.m.							
12:00 p.m.							
1:00 p.m.							
2:00 p.m.							
3:00 p.m.							
4:00 p.m.							
5:00 p.m.							
6:00 p.m.							
7:00 p.m.							
8:00 p.m.							
9:00 p.m.							
10:00 p.m.							
11:00 p.m.							

4. Look at your list and commit to always having reading materials with you so that you can take advantage of these times.

5. Reexamine the breaks in your teaching year (e.g., fall break, winter break, spring break, and summer break). Make a plan to use at least some of this time for your writing project. Ask a friend to join you in your plan and hold each other accountable.

4

Bust Your Writing-Related Myths

Many myths keep students and scholars from writing, and they can paralyze writers when they aren't recognized as myths. Some of them—like never end a sentence with a preposition or never use a split infinitive—focus on style or sentence structure. People who struggle with those myths, however, are already writing, and that is a good thing. In this chapter, we want to help people overcome the myths that keep them from writing in the first place or that keep them from attempting to publish work they have written. While we recognize that there are more writing-related myths than these, we will focus on the following ones: the magnum opus delusion, the impostor syndrome, the cleared deck fantasy, the one more source seduction, and the stronger credentials fallacy.[1] We have chosen these myths because they have, at times, embedded themselves in our own brains, and these are the myths that we see stifling our students and colleagues.

Virginia Woolf, one of the greatest writers and critics of the twentieth century, realized she had "to do battle with a certain phantom"

1. These are adapted from Joli Jensen, *Write No Matter What: Advice for Academics* (Chicago: University of Chicago Press, 2017), 39–74.

in order to write. But she was able to kill that phantom in self-defense, explaining, "Had I not killed her, she would have killed me. She would have plucked the heart out of my writing."[2] The phantom Woolf battled is a myth similar to the impostor syndrome and the stronger credentials fallacy. Woolf explains that it is difficult to kill something of a fictitious nature because "it is far harder to kill a phantom than a reality."[3] The phantom can come back to life, and Woolf laments that "the struggle was severe; it took much time that had better have been spent upon learning Greek grammar; or in roaming the world in search of adventures."[4] We hope that this chapter helps you do battle with and destroy the writing myth that works to pluck the heart out of your writing. We often fail to write and publish when we allow these writing myths to go unchecked.

MYTH #1: MAGNUM OPUS DELUSION

The magnum opus delusion tricks you into believing that if you don't produce the most influential masterpiece, then you are simply wasting your time. If it's not a magnum opus, you might as well pack your bags and go home. It is the yearning of a student or scholar to write something so magnificent that it cannot be ignored by others in the field. But such thinking can not only paralyze us; it can also leave us riddled with guilt and shame for failing to produce such a work. Jensen explains, "The magnum opus myth misleads all of us into believing that competence is not enough, that our project needs to be the most influential or impressive work in the field, now and forevermore. This delusion is not true or useful to believe."[5]

Jensen argues that it is "better to think of our work as our current contribution to an ongoing conversation."[6] We don't need to produce a magnum opus that transforms our discipline. We only need to move the conversation forward. When I (Adrianne) was working on my

2. Virginia Woolf, "Professions for Women," in *The Death of the Moth, and Other Essays* (Harmondsworth, UK: Penguin, 1961), 202, 203.
3. Woolf, "Professions for Women," 203.
4. Woolf, "Professions for Women," 203.
5. Jensen, *Write No Matter What*, 48.
6. Jensen, *Write No Matter What*, 48.

PhD, I wrote a journal article, which grew out of a course research paper on Southern Paiute final features. I do not speak Southern Paiute, and this article was not a magnum opus on Southern Paiute phonology. Additionally, this article was not directly related to my dissertation. Had I believed I must make a major contribution to studies in the Numic branch of Uto-Aztecan or studies in optimality theory, I would have stopped myself from working on this paper beyond the required coursework. However, my phonology professor was particularly good at communicating to his students that our job was to move the conversation forward, not speak the final word. Because I chose to believe him instead of the magnum opus delusion, I moved the conversation concerning final features as morphophonological alternations forward in a small but (we like to think) helpful way.

MYTH #2: IMPOSTOR SYNDROME

The impostor syndrome causes students and scholars to believe that they have fooled people into thinking they are legitimate, but secretly they think that they are merely impostors. Somehow, they made it into an MA, ThM, DMin, or PhD program (or even through the PhD program), which was a great accomplishment. But now, if they write and attempt to submit a dissertation chapter to their supervising professor or attempt to publish an article or book, they fear being exposed as a fraud. Even for someone who has successfully published material, there is a tendency to feel inadequate and believe previous publications were just flukes and that our next project will reveal to everyone that we don't belong in academia. Jensen comments, "It is not shameful to feel inadequate. It is normal, widespread, and connected to our yearning to be the kind of academic who earns respect."[7]

We need to remember that writing is about contributing to our field; it's not about us. Yes, it takes courage to write and submit our work for our professor's or publisher's review, knowing that some may criticize it. But nobody has fully arrived, and we need humility to continue to learn and grow. When the impostor syndrome rears

7. Jensen, *Write No Matter What*, 53.

its ugly head, cut it off. Remind yourself that intelligent, respected individuals admitted you to the program of study or conferred your degree on you. Remember the good work you have done, and don't minimize it. Speak truth in grace to yourself. Also rightly consider the feedback you've been given. Criticism or feedback from an instructor, colleague, or publisher is not an indication that you really are an impostor. Feedback is not judgment. It is analysis. When a colleague in your field takes the time to offer sound criticism, welcome it (as difficult as that may be) and use it to improve your work. Criticism is not confirmation that you're an impostor any more than physical exercise is confirmation of physical weakness. Both are processes that result in a stronger product in the end, either stronger writing or stronger muscles.

When an article I (Adrianne) submitted for publication was rejected, the reviewer's comments hurt my ego. I could have believed the myth that I was a fraud in my field and had no business continuing to work in this field, and honestly, the thought crossed my mind. But I chose to remember the positive feedback I had received over the years, and I chose to believe that my current research would be a valuable contribution to the scholarly conversation. The reviewer who rejected the proposed article told me to do more with less. (I had not moved the conversation forward despite having analyzed what turned out to be too much data.) After nursing my bruised ego, I had to admit that the reviewer wasn't wrong. I reworked the paper taking those comments into consideration and ended up with two papers that are much better than that first extra-long, overly full, somewhat weak paper. One of those articles has been published in an academic journal, and the other one is currently in a working draft stage and will be submitted for publication consideration.

Recently, I (Ben) sent in a completed book manuscript to two well-known scholars who serve as editors for a series. I had doubts as to whether they would accept and approve my work. Although I was invited to contribute to the series because I have published on that particular topic, I still wondered how they would respond to my work. Why were they taking so long to respond to me? Had they already read the manuscript? If so, why hadn't they contacted me and congratulated me on my good work? Or maybe they were just too busy to read it. Yes (I tried to convince myself), that must be the answer. (The manuscript was eventually accepted, and all was well.) Doubt is real and the impostor syndrome is real. But most of the time we really have nothing to worry about, and so we create unnecessary anxiety. As someone once told me, "Don't cross the bridge before you get to it, or you'll end up paying double toll."

MYTH #3: CLEARED DECK FANTASY

The cleared deck fantasy is embraced by those well-intentioned people who state that they want, plan, and intend to write, but only after they first free themselves of all other obligations. They will write soon, once they complete their to-do list. They need to clear the deck before sitting down to write. They remain on the verge of producing something significant but can only complete it within the ideal block of time that, unfortunately, is elusive. Jensen reminds us, "The point is that *things never clear up*. They don't even reliably settle down. Our inbox is always full. Our decks are always crowded. There is always more going on than we expect."[8] Waiting for a cleared deck removes us from our writing project, and the longer we are away from a project, the harder it is to reengage. Writing becomes another item on the to-do list, an item that keeps getting moved to the bottom of the list. If writing is merely an obligation and not a privilege, it will never receive the priority that it deserves.

Think of writing as a privilege, not as a chore. It is a way to organize your thoughts and opinions. When writing becomes a time of refuge or a place of solace, then we will more diligently pursue it. As discussed below in chapter 6, serious writers must develop the habit of writing. When writing is a habit, just another part of your day, you won't feel the need to clear the deck before writing. As with other habits, you'll just do it. For example, you don't feel the need to clean the bathroom before brushing your teeth each morning because brushing your teeth is a habit, not a special task. Make writing a habit and see it as a privilege; then your need to clear the deck will diminish.

8. Jensen, *Write No Matter What*, 57.

As we write this chapter, our decks are not cleared. I (Adrianne) have twenty-four British literature essays to grade, twenty-one final project prospectuses and annotated bibliographies to review for my writing class, twenty-one abstracts and query letters to grade, a dissertation to evaluate, and three articles to review—all before the week is out. And I (Ben) have a PhD oral defense to attend, a DMin project to read, emails to answer, classes to prepare for, PowerPoints to revise, and papers to grade. If we had waited until our decks were clear, this book would never have been written. Writing this book is a privilege because it gives us the opportunity to articulate our thoughts and experiences on writing in ways that will help others embrace writing and hone their skills. To be completely honest, this process also helps us become better writers. It's a blessing that we must consciously choose to prioritize. We will get to our grading, reviewing, and other tasks, but if we always put those things first, believing we need a cleared deck to write, dedicated writing time will forever elude us.

MYTH #4: ONE MORE SOURCE SEDUCTION

One more source is the myth that says you can't begin writing until you have read all your sources and know exactly what you are going to say. And you can't know what you are going to say until you have examined every source on your topic. So it is best not to start the writing process until your reading is complete. But this line of thinking is unhelpful. Of course, you can begin writing too early. You need some knowledge of the topic you are pursuing. Michael Kibbe warns, "Don't start writing your paper too soon."[9] However, we have found that writing too soon is seldom the problem. Anne Huff offers a helpful balance: "If you begin writing too soon, your thinking may be so embryonic that you do not find the effort very clarifying. If you wait too long to write, you are likely to have so many ideas they are difficult to organize and express clearly."[10] Most academics we know err on the side of waiting too long (especially those who are perfectionists).

---

9. Michael Kibbe, *From Topic to Thesis: A Guide to Theological Research* (Downers Grove, IL: InterVarsity, 2016), 88.

10. Anne Sigismund Huff, *Writing for Scholarly Publication* (Thousand Oaks, CA: Sage, 1999), 8.

Don't attempt to read everything first and only later begin the writing process. Why? First, there are always more articles and books to read or consult. If the reading never stops, then the writing never starts. Jensen explains, "It feels easier and safer to be 'researching' rather than doing the hard and sometimes scary work of writing. Background research keeps us from feeling anxious, but when it goes on too long it is a form of stalling."[11] Second, you will inevitably forget what you read and where you read it. This will cause a researcher to continually need to reread material and waste precious time trying to recall valuable information. Third, the more you read, the more overwhelmed you will become. You must have an outlet to release the pressure of retaining that much knowledge. Roy Peter Clark identifies the problem: "Many writers use research to fill up available time. Thorough exploration makes writing seem tougher. Write earlier in the process so you discover what information you need."[12]

As I (Ben) read, I use a highlighter and pen to mark up the material that I'm reading. When I'm done reading that chapter (or perhaps a few chapters), I summarize the material and take notes. Similarly, I (Adrianne) underline as I read and make comments in the margins of the text. I also use sticky notes to record comments in books I read because I like to read on the couch or outside, where holding a notebook or laptop is cumbersome. Every morning, I transcribe my markups and sticky notes into a Word document so that I can easily search and find the information I need as I write.

Writing down your thoughts helps you crystallize your position or argumentation. As we write, we often gain clarity and insight on concepts that are cloudy in our minds. Specifically related to this last point of writing earlier in the process, it is advantageous to produce an outline of your essay or chapter as early as possible. Otherwise, when you gather material in your research, it all goes into the same collection of facts and insights and quotes. Soon that grows from a small pail to a five-gallon bucket filled to the brim and seemingly unmanageable. Starting with an outline allows a person to drop information into

11. Jensen, *Write No Matter What*, 72.
12. Roy Peter Clark, *Writing Tools: 55 Essential Strategies for Every Writer* (New York: Little, Brown, 2016), 203.

smaller containers that can be easily grasped and manipulated. For example, in writing this book, my (Ben's) first step was to jot down the most helpful practices and principles that aid in my ability to write. Once I settled on twelve containers and began reading on the topic of writing, any helpful information gained was placed in the appropriate bucket.[13] I (Adrianne) also develop an outline early in my research and writing process. My outline may change as my research continues, but I start with a color-coded outline, and I color-code my notes as I read to coordinate them with my outline topics. Eventually, the same-colored text will be grouped together and serve as the scaffolding for a first draft.

In summary, don't wait too long to write. Write as you research. It will save time in the long run, allowing you to finish your essay or book or degree more quickly.

MYTH #5: STRONGER CREDENTIALS FALLACY

Somewhat related to the one more source myth and the impostor syndrome is the stronger credentials fallacy. Would-be writers sometimes wait to write or put off trying to publish their work under the fallacious assumption that they will be in a better position to write and publish once they earn their next credential. A graduate student may fool herself into thinking she should wait until she earns her degree to write a journal article and submit it for publication or to send a query letter about writing a book review or even a book proposal. A junior faculty member may erroneously believe he needs to get a few more years of experience under his belt or be invited to be a plenary speaker before systematically writing with the goal of publishing his work.

The truth of the matter is that all academics who are actively involved in research are experts (or at least are becoming experts) in their field. We may not be experts in the most general understanding of that term, but we are experts in our own little corners (or large corners) of scholarship. My (Adrianne's) dissertation committee chair

---

13. Anne Huff maintains that an outline "provides directions that reduce the need for constant inspiration as writing proceeds." *Writing for Scholarly Publication*, 77.

told me early in my dissertation research that he expected me to become an expert on my topic. He expected me to know more about that specific topic than he knew. At first, this idea seemed impossible to me. He was an associate professor at a top research university and had been working in this field for many years. How would I ever know more about anything than he knew? As I continued to research and write, I grew to understand the truth of his words. He was not researching in my specific corner of scholarship. He knew more about phonology—especially the phonology of African languages—than I would ever know, but he did not know more about the phonology of signed languages. Instead, he encouraged me to educate him on sign language phonology, which was incredibly helpful in the writing of my dissertation. The realization that I was an expert in my specific area gave me the confidence to present aspects of my research at the Northeastern Linguistics Society Conference and at the Seventh International Conference on Theoretical Issues in Sign Language Research. However, instead of transforming these conference talks into articles for publication, I focused on finishing my dissertation as quickly as possible. In hindsight, I wish I would have dedicated time and effort to publish those works. The best way to combat the stronger credentials fallacy is to recognize it for what it is—a myth—and to recognize yourself for who you are—an expert in your specific area of research.

CONCLUSION

Recognizing the myths that keep you from writing is the first step toward overcoming them. Whatever myth hinders you from moving forward with your writing must be identified and defeated. You must do battle with your "phantoms" as Virginia Woolf did with hers. The choice is simple: kill them or they will kill the writer in you. This battle may have to be fought many times, because our phantoms, our myths, have a way of coming back to life again and again. Do not affirm the myths. Do not let them get a foothold. Combat them and destroy them (daily if needed) so that you can write. You have something to say; don't let phantoms keep you from saying it.

THE NEXT LEVEL

We have discussed and busted the magnum opus delusion, the impostor syndrome, the cleared deck fantasy, the one more source seduction, and the stronger credentials fallacy. While these are real issues that plague writers, we do not have to be constrained by them. The following questions are designed to help you identify and bust the myths that are keeping you from contributing to the scholarly conversation.

1. Magnum Opus Delusion
   a. Do you think that because your work is not a magnum opus, it is not worth writing or publishing?
   b. Describe one aspect of your research that would move the scholarly conversation in your field forward. If you are struggling with the magnum opus delusion, discuss your answer to this question with a colleague or mentor. Seek and accept honest feedback.

_____

_____

_____

_____

2. Impostor Syndrome
   a. List one thing you don't know or understand but believe you should know or understand. Look at your answer and honestly tell yourself whether that one thing discredits all your other insights and accomplishments.
   b. List your accomplishments. If you are a graduate student, list every good grade you've earned. Reread the positive comments from your instructors. If you are a professional academic, list every degree you've earned, every academic job you've held, and every scholarly activity you've participated

in (e.g., conferences, panel discussions, blog posts, articles). Read this list (or read your CV) and speak the truth to yourself—you are not an impostor.

-----

3. Cleared Deck Fantasy
    a. What tasks do you absolutely have to complete each day? This list is likely shorter than you imagined.
    b. Set a thirty-minute or one-hour timer in the morning and complete these tasks. When the timer goes off, stop the task, even if you are not finished. Then set a one-hour timer and write. Write an outline, write notes from reading, write a paragraph—just write. When the timer goes off, make a few notes about where you will pick up with this work tomorrow, and then go back to your regular to-do list. Practice this technique for a week and see what happens.

-----

4. One More Source Seduction
    a. How many sources have you read for your research? If you have read more than six, it is time to draft an outline (if you haven't already). Continue to read as you add details to your outline. Be willing to edit your outline as you gain more

insight. When your outline grows longer than one page, it is time to start drafting your paper. Your outline can continue to grow, but it's time to write some paragraphs.

b. Describe your system for taking notes as you read and research. If you have not developed a system, describe what you are going to start doing. If you are looking for a better way to take notes and organize them, there's an app for that. Although we prefer the tried-and-true word processing app, we've heard good things about the Ulysses app.

5. Stronger Credentials Fallacy

a. List all your academic credentials (e.g., accepted into a graduate program, every good grade you earned, all academic jobs held, all honors or awards). Read this list and recognize the work you've put into becoming an expert in your area of research.

b. Describe the area of research for which you are an expert. This may be a very narrow area (like the phonology of handshape in American Sign Language), but you need to realize that you are an expert, and you have something to contribute to this area.

5

Don't Wait to Write

What do painters do? They paint. They do it because they love it or feel compelled to do it. What do musicians do? They create and play music. They do it because they love it or feel compelled to do it. And what do writers do? They write.[1] If you want to write, it means you must become a writer. Writers write. Whether you are a college student, a graduate student, or a faculty member, if you want to be a writer, write. Don't be a mercenary writer, only writing when there's a cash reward. You will never finish your degree if you wait for the perfect time to write, and you will never become an established writer if you wait to get invited to write a blog post, to contribute an essay to a journal or edited volume, or to get a contract from a well-known publisher. Write because you have something to say.

STOP MAKING EXCUSES

In the previous chapter, we discussed several writing-related myths that keep writers from writing. Those myths can be categorized under

1. As Natalie Goldberg says, "If you want to write, write." *Wild Mind: Living the Writer's Life* (New York: Bantam, 1990), 45. For books on the life of a writer, see Dorothea Brande, *Becoming a Writer* (New York: Tarcher/Putnam, 1934); Natalie Goldberg, *Writing Down the Bones: Freeing the Writer Within* (Boston: Shambhala 2005); Brenda Ueland, *If You Want to Write* (1938; repr., Mansfield Centre, CT: Martino, 2011); and Jeff Goins, *You Are a Writer: So Start Acting like One* (Columbia, SC: Tribe, 2012).

the broader notions of procrastination and self-doubt. Both are enemies that writers must work to slay again and again throughout their
careers. These enemies do not always appear as the writing myths
we've already discussed. Often they capitalize on the busyness of life
to keep you from writing now.

Such is the method of procrastination. Whether you are a student
or a professional, you are busy. Students have multiple assignments
vying for their time. Many also work to support themselves. Some
have families, and all (should) have social lives to keep them emotionally healthy and well-balanced. In addition, Christian writers serve
their churches in a variety of ways. Time is a limited resource, but
procrastination leads you to believe that you will have time tomorrow, next week, next month, definitely next year. These are lies. You
will never have more time, and you cannot *make* time. Instead, you
must *redeem* the time you have, as we discussed in chapter 3. But
you can't redeem your time if you allow yourself to believe the lies
of procrastination. Instead, follow the example of Jesus: speak the
truth in love to yourself. If you have thirty minutes for lunch, instead
of eating in the break room with your friends, work on the outline
for your paper (or book). You can have your lunch *and* get some
writing done with a small adjustment to your schedule. Instead of
procrastinating, be productive.

Helen Sword says, "Productivity, I discovered, is a broad church
that tolerates many creeds,"[2] and we agree. Some writers are most
productive if they write at least a little bit every day. Others do better
by writing in larger chunks of time a few sessions a week. While we
realize some seasons of life push writing to the margins of school
breaks, we encourage writers to write often and regularly, at least on
a weekly basis. This keeps your research fresh in your mind and your
train of thought going. Robert Boice likens not writing regularly
(for him daily) to "backsliding."[3] In other words, once you are out
of the habit of writing regularly, it can be difficult to get back into
it. However, do not allow the guilt of not writing regularly keep you

2. Helen Sword, *Air & Light & Time & Space: How Successful Academics Write*
(Cambridge, MA: Harvard University Press, 2017), 15.
3. Robert Boice, *Professors as Writers: A Self-Help Guide to Productive Writing*,
4th ed. (Stillwater, OK: New Forums, 1990), 121.

from writing. Procrastination can often lead to guilt, which can be more paralyzing than the procrastinating tendency itself. Eliminate "should have" from your thinking and replace it with "can."[4] Instead of saying to yourself that you should have taken advantage of the canceled faculty meeting and spent that hour writing, tell yourself that you can block out four to five this Tuesday for writing. Prioritize that appointment and keep it. Small steps toward productivity create productivity. Do not let procrastination or guilt win the day. Write! Do it today and don't put it off until the perfect tomorrow that seldom comes. Be productive with the time you have worked to redeem. The grading, the laundry, or whatever other task is screaming, "Take care of me instead of writing!" will still get done if you prioritize writing. Your writing will not get done if you continue to procrastinate.

The other big roadblock keeping many academics from writing is self-doubt. Have you earned the right to say anything at all about your topic? The answer is *yes*, you have! Don't believe the lies that you are not good enough, smart enough, or well-read enough to have something to say. Don't believe that what you have to say isn't worth saying. You have done the research, and you have a contribution (no matter how small) to add to the conversation. Don't allow self-doubt to take you out of the game before you even get in.

We will talk more about soliciting and using feedback in chapters 8 and 9. The feedback you receive may be harsh. Sometimes it might feed your self-doubt, but you must work against that. Responding to feedback will make your work stronger in the long run. I (Adrianne) live in a house full of athletes, and I think a sports analogy is apt for thinking about self-doubt and writing. Let the feedback you solicit call the "time-out." Use that time-out to regroup and formulate a better game plan. Learn from the different coaches who comment on your work, but don't take yourself out of the game because of your own self-doubt.

If procrastination or self-doubt hounds you, take steps to slay this enemy. Speak the truth in love to yourself about your time and your writing. Ask a friend to hold you accountable regarding the times

---

4. Sword offers a similar argument for replacing "should" with "may." *Air & Light & Time & Space*, 42.

you've redeemed for writing and ask them to help you be honest with yourself about what you have to say. When I (Adrianne) had an article rejected for publication by one journal, my encouraging colleague told me it was a good article that would find an audience, but that journal just wasn't the right one. Without that encouragement, I might have shelved that article, and all the hours I put into it would have been wasted. Instead, I allowed the reviewers' comments to "coach" me rather than take me out of the game. I revised and submitted that article to another journal, where it was accepted for publication. However you do it, combat your writing enemies! Don't let them win. Instead, write and keep writing!

FIND YOUR SPACE

Two other enemies of writing are clutter and distraction. In order to write regularly, it is a helpful practice to create a space that is as free as possible of the things that distract you. Stephen King recommends what he calls "closed door" writing.[5] He explains that you need a space with a door that you can close, "and you need the determination to shut the door."[6] Shutting the door, both literally and figuratively, shuts out the distractions and allows you to do the kind of work that Eviatar Zerubavel classifies as "A-time" writing—focused creation of sentences and paragraphs.[7]

Think critically about the spaces you have. Can you close the door of your office and write? If the answer is yes, great. Keep the writing appointments you have set. My (Adrianne's) office is not near any classrooms, so the foot traffic I get is limited to colleagues. I recognize that "watercooler" talk can rob me of valuable writing time, so during my writing times I shut the door. Thankfully, few people knock on a closed door in my building. For some of you, though, the office is too busy for writing. You might shut your door, but it won't stay shut. If that is the case for you, find another space for writing. One of our

5. Stephen King, *On Writing: A Memoir of the Craft* (New York: Scribner, 2000), 155.

6. King, *On Writing*, 157.

7. Eviatar Zerubavel, *The Clockwork Muse: A Practical Guide to Writing Theses, Dissertations, and Books* (Cambridge, MA: Harvard University Press, 1999), 34.

colleagues writes in the school cafeteria. While that would be too distracting for me, my friend pops in her earbuds—the equivalent of shutting her door—opens her laptop, and writes with books spread out on the table. No one bothers her. She looks busy, and she is.

Some of our friends find that writing at home is the best way to get closed-door writing time. They may have home offices or use a bedroom, back porch, or laundry room—whatever works is a good space for writing. Many academics forget that each campus has a quiet place for writing that is free of many distractions—the school library. Most libraries have carrels you can rent or claim on a first-come basis. Take advantage of those quiet stacks where few people linger. No office phones, no emails, no watercooler talk to distract you, just rows of books to inspire you to put your head down and write. As you think critically about the best writing space for you, don't be afraid to experiment. Try your office. If you can't keep the door shut, try a different space. Don't give up. Keep trying until you find the space that works for you, the space that enables productivity.

WRITE BEFORE THE PATH IS CLEAR

Productivity seldom, if ever, means that you sit down to write already knowing everything you want to say. If you wait until you know everything, you will never write anything. King explains that "writing is refined thinking."[8] As you continue to research your topic, begin writing. You may write out questions that you have and write in the answers or hypothesized answers as you research. Allow these questions and answers to develop into an outline for your paper or book. But don't get hung up on the word "outline." This word can stifle the best writers at times. Instead, think of designing a road map that will lead your readers from questions to answers or from problems to solutions. As you refine your thinking through writing, you will refine your questions and answers and narrow your focus to create a working draft. We will talk more about drafting and soliciting feedback in the following chapters, but for now, we want you to grasp the importance of writing near the beginning of your research path.

8. King, *On Writing*, 131.

In some ways, students have an advantage over faculty when it comes to writing along the path. Because students are required to take various classes and because many (if not most) graduate-level classes require some kind of research paper, forward-thinking students may choose to connect their various class papers to the research topic of interest that will become their thesis or dissertation. We are not saying that a dissertation is simply the stapling together of a half dozen class papers, although I (Adrianne) admit that I daydreamed about such possibilities as a graduate student. We are saying that class papers may become dissertation chapters or foundations for those chapters. And we are encouraging students to connect their coursework to their thesis or dissertation whenever possible. Not only does this get you writing along the path; it also provides valuable feedback from a variety of professors.

Junior faculty members also have a bit of an advantage because they recently defended a dissertation. They are already on a writing path and can transform their dissertation into several journal articles or a monograph. The challenge is to redeem the time, amid new job responsibilities, to continue writing. We also encourage you to keep a file of new writing-project ideas. As you work to publish all or part of your dissertation, you will think of other questions and other avenues of research. You think you will never forget those ideas, but after a few hundred graded papers you might forget your own name. Keep a file of those ideas that you can go back to for future writing projects. It's better to have too many potential projects than none at all.

For academics who have published all they can from their dissertation, mine your idea file or look to the courses you are teaching. Do you find yourself supplementing the available material with your own (possibly extensive) handouts? Do you read through your textbook choices and wish there were a text that approached the subject in a new way? If so, start writing your own textbook or supplemental text. Remember, academics do not write for the money—academic publishing is not a lucrative field. We write because we believe we have something helpful to say. I (Ben) had my first (nondissertation) book nearly completed before I received a contract from a publisher. It is nearly impossible to get your first (and sometimes second) book published. But I believed that even if I didn't find a publisher, the material I was developing would be useful for my teaching and thus for my students.

As you continue in your academic career, be alert to the needs in your field. Are there questions unanswered, analyses or assumptions unchallenged? Academic writers believe that through years of diligent study, we can correct misunderstandings, repackage well-known topics for a new generation, or employ new methods that challenge or confirm established convictions. Part of my (Ben's) dissertation was written to correct misunderstandings about the office of elder in the early church. That work led to the publication of an academic monograph and to a question-and-answer book for popular audiences. As a professor of New Testament Greek, I have also written books to help students of Greek. There are many Greek texts on the market, but I repackaged this topic by making readers aware of the "insight that knowing Greek grammar can bring," by "summariz[ing] thirty-five key Greek grammatical issues and their significance for interpreting the New Testament."[9] Over the years, I have not written (primarily) to get published, promoted, or praised (or even to get my degrees). Rather, I—and academics in general—write because we believe that we can contribute to the conversation in our field of research and teaching.

START SMALL AND GROW

Writing as you go means that you do not instantaneously complete a forty-thousand-word text. But it does mean that you write regularly. We will address the importance of making writing a habit in the next chapter. Here, we want you to think about the kinds of works you may write. As you are working toward a thesis, dissertation, journal article, or book, do not miss opportunities to write and publish texts on your project topic as you go.

Students may find opportunities for writing or publishing in various writing contests. The relatively small school where we work offers writing contests at the graduate and undergraduate levels.

9. Benjamin L. Merkle, *Exegetical Gems from Biblical Greek: A Refreshing Guide to Grammar and Interpretation* (Grand Rapids: Baker Academic, 2019), back cover.

A few of these contests offer cash prizes for the winners, and one includes publication in an academic journal. Look for similar contests at your school. Graduate students are often encouraged to present their work at conferences, and we discuss the importance of conference participation in chapter 10. Keep in mind that many conferences have contests for student papers. I (Adrianne) had no idea these kinds of contests existed until my thesis director encouraged me to apply. I was pleasantly surprised to win the award, with a little bit of prize money, and have my paper published in the journal proceedings from the conference. That publication was part of my thesis and was written and published before my thesis was complete. We stress to students that they should write as they go and look for opportunities to publish aspects of their larger, ongoing work.

Another great venue for starting small and sharing some of your work is in blogging. Many blogs are for popular audiences, and there is nothing wrong with packaging your research for general readers. In fact, this is a great skill for instructors. We also encourage you to seek out scholarly blogs that are well regarded in your field and inquire about how you might contribute.

Many academics see the monograph as the golden goose of publication. We've already warned you that there is no golden goose in academic writing, but if you want to write academic books, we suggest that you begin by writing book reviews (which is also a good way to get free books). Again, work to align your small steps with your larger writing goals. Review books that contribute to your project research when possible. After you have success writing book reviews, move on to publishing essays in academic journals. When you present your work at a conference, investigate publishing an article in the conference proceedings. Some conference proceedings are refereed— a feather in your academic publishing cap. If you find a particular journal popping up again and again in your research, you know the kind of work they publish. Develop an article and submit it to that journal.

Starting small and being an active writer will help you when you are ready to publish a book. Trying to publish your first book is a catch-22. You can't get a contract to publish a book until you have already published a book. But if a publisher sees that you aggressively publish book reviews and journal articles, they will look at your request for a contract more favorably. They will see you as a writer who stays current in your field and who is dedicated to contributing to your area of expertise. In other words, they will see a writer who writes, and as we and many others have said, if you want to be a writer, you must write.

REWARD YOURSELF

We know that writing is hard work. We know that there are other things vying for your time because writing is not your full-time job. When people persevere in challenging tasks, they tend to reward themselves. After a good workout, you get a protein drink or a sports drink. When your team wins the tournament, you go out to celebrate. When your office group finishes a project, you all receive a bonus. Don't let writing become unrewarded work. It's challenging enough already. Without some built-in rewards, you might find it harder and harder to prioritize. Your rewards do not have to be spectacular; they just have to work for you. If you are like me (Adrianne), food is a reward that puts a smile on your face. My regular writing goal is five hundred words a day. Tempting snacks sit on the shelf beside my desk, but I do not get a snack until I've reached my five-hundred-word goal. A piece of dark chocolate or a snack bag of Cheetos is a great reward in my book. One of my colleagues grants himself a leisurely stroll around campus on pleasant days after he's put in his writing time for the day. Others indulge in watercooler conversations as their reward. As with so many aspects of writing, you have to find what works for you. We encourage you to not use as a reward something that you enjoy several times a day regardless of what you do. If I ate Cheetos for breakfast, lunch, and dinner, they wouldn't be much of a reward. Your writing reward should be something special that is just associated with completing your regular writing tasks. Leaving your writing project with a smile on your face will (hopefully) enable you to pick it back up with a smile on your face. We know that we ultimately write because we have something meaningful to say, but a little reward never hurts.

CONCLUSION

You want to be an academic writer. Otherwise, you would not be reading this book. We hope this chapter has encouraged and equipped you to start writing right now. There is no perfect time to begin writing, so don't wait for it. Do it now. Make your contributions to your field. No one else has your unique insights or your particular approach to your subject matter. Recognize the excuses you've been making and shut them down. Talk to the people around you who get excited about what you have to say. Join the conversation. Write! Don't wait!

THE NEXT LEVEL

1. What tasks push your writing further down on your to-do list?

2. What changes can you make to your schedule today (or this week) to prioritize your writing over the tasks you listed in the question above?

3. Who can be your writing encourager (e.g., your spouse, friend, or colleague)? Write that person's name down and talk to them

today. Be straightforward and ask them to regularly inquire about your writing and regularly encourage you to write.

_____

_____

_____

4. Do you have an outline, road map, or questions with potential answers for your current writing project? If not, block out thirty minutes this week when you can focus and write your road map.

_____

_____

_____

5. Brainstorm ideas for future writing projects and save them in one file so that you can easily find them and add to them in the future.

6. List a few options for small-step publications as you work on your larger project. Where can you blog, write a book review, or contribute an article that reflects some part of your ongoing research? List these options out and make a plan to pursue at least one of them.

_____

_____

_____

6

Make Writing a Habit

Nearly every accomplished writer or artist is successful (at least in part) because they developed the discipline and daily habit of practicing their skill. In this chapter, we want to help you understand the importance of developing your own writing habits. We will review the habits of famous writers and artists, along with their attitudes about those habits. We will also share our own failures and successes and offer tips for developing good writing habits that work for you. Hopefully, these habits will move you from being just a well-intentioned writer to being a consistent and productive one.

THE HABITS OF WRITERS

In his book *Daily Rituals: How Artists Work*, Mason Currey details the routines of 161 artists.[1] We often think that true writers or artists write or perform their art only when they feel inspired and creative. But what Currey's book reveals is that such thinking is completely false. Although there was great diversity in the daily routines of those surveyed, one consistent feature is that they kept a (usually strict) schedule to perform their craft. They were successful to the extent that they kept to their daily routines.

1. Mason Currey, *Daily Rituals: How Artists Work* (New York: Knopf, 2013).

Listen to the testimony of artists who excelled in their craft:

- John Adams (b. 1947): "My experience has been that most really serious creative people I know have very, very routine and not particularly glamorous work habits." He continues, "I find basically that if I do things regularly, I don't have writer's block or come into terrible crises."[2]
- Leo Tolstoy (1828–1910): "I must write each day without fail, not so much for the success of the work, as in order not to get out of my routine."[3]
- John Updike (1932–2009): "I think that the pleasures of not writing are so great that if you ever start indulging them you will never write again. . . . [A solid routine] saves you from giving up."[4]

In addition to the actual words of the authors mentioned above, Currey summarizes the routines of those in his survey.

- Francis Bacon (1909–1992): "He was 'essentially a creature of habit' with a daily schedule that varied little over his career."[5]
- Henry Miller (1891–1980): "Two or three hours in the morning were enough for him, although he stressed the importance of keeping regular hours in order to cultivate a daily creative rhythm."[6]
- Andy Warhol (1928–1987): "Keeping to his beloved weekday 'rut' was so important to Andy that he veered from it only when he was forced to."[7]

Stephen King also believes in maintaining a disciplined schedule, including a daily word count. He states, "Once I start work on a project, I don't stop and I don't slow down unless I absolutely have to."

2. Currey, *Daily Rituals*, 65, 66.
3. Currey, *Daily Rituals*, 169.
4. Currey, *Daily Rituals*, 196.
5. Currey, *Daily Rituals*, 5.
6. Currey, *Daily Rituals*, 53.
7. Currey, *Daily Rituals*, 189.

He adds, "The truth is that when I'm writing, I write every day. . . . That *includes* Christmas, the Fourth, and my birthday. . . . Only under dire circumstances do I allow myself to shut down before I get to my 2,000 words."[8]

TIME: A SUCCESSFUL HABIT

In his classic work, *On Writing Well*, William Zinsser asserts, "The professional writer must establish a daily schedule and stick to it. . . . Writing is a craft, not an art, and the man who runs away from his craft because he lacks inspiration is fooling himself."[9] He later adds, "You learn to write by writing. . . . The only way to learn to write is to force yourself to produce a certain number of words on a regular basis."[10]

My (Ben's) friend Robert Plummer puts it this way: "If you sit there, it will come." Some of us remember the baseball movie *Field of Dreams*, starring Kevin Costner. The most important line in the movie was "If you build it, [they] will come."[11] If Costner's character would build a baseball field on his farm, then Shoeless Joe Jackson and other former players who had died would come. Likewise, if you build a habit of sitting down for extended periods of time, then words and sentences and paragraphs and pages will come. Unless you actually spend time devoted to writing, it will be difficult to write.

In response to the question of how she writes, author Anne Lamott responds, "You sit down, I say. You try to sit down at approximately the same time every day. . . . I wish I felt that kind of inspiration more often. I almost never do. All I know is that if I sit there long enough, something will happen. . . . So much of writing is about sitting down and doing it every day."[12] Unfortunately, many students and beginning

---

8. Stephen King, *On Writing: A Memoir of the Craft* (New York: Scribner, 2000), 153, 154. See also Currey, *Daily Rituals*, 224.

9. William Zinsser, *On Writing Well: The Classic Guide to Writing Nonfiction*, 7th ed., rev. and updated (New York: Harper Perennial, 2006), 4.

10. Zinsser, *On Writing Well*, 49.

11. The actual quote has "he" rather than "they" (referring to Shoeless Joe Jackson, and then by implication the other former players who died). *Field of Dreams*, directed by Phil Alden Robinson (Universal City, CA: Universal Pictures, 1989).

12. Anne Lamott, *Bird by Bird: Some Instructions on Writing and Life*, 2nd ed. (New York: Anchor, 2019), 6, 9, 142.

writers are easily distracted—sometimes seeming to look for distractions so that they won't have to do the hard work of writing.

One thing is certain: if you don't sit in front of your computer or tablet or notebook, you won't be able to produce work. If you get up from your desk every ten minutes to get coffee—which then leads to a lengthy conversation or to checking social media—then the writing will suffer. You need undistracted time when you do nothing but write.[13] If finding and protecting undistracted time seems a bit overwhelming, you don't have to do this alone. As with many things in the twenty-first century, there's an app for that. A quick internet search for "apps for staying focused on work" yields over three billion results. There are apps for your phone and your computer that allow you to block distracting apps during set periods. You control what is blocked by selecting the things that distract you (e.g., email, social media, texts, or other instant messages). These apps are designed to help you build better habits, and many of them are free. Take advantage of technology that inhibits distractions.

As we discussed in chapter 1, writing is hard work. If it were easy, more people would do it. But like anything that requires hours and hours, the careful selecting and placing of words on a page takes its toll on the body and the mind. Philip Roth states, "Writing isn't hard work, it's a nightmare. . . . Coal mining is hard work. This is a nightmare. . . . A good writer is locked in a battle with his work. . . . One skill that every writer needs is the ability to sit still in this deeply uneventful business."[14] Many students and potential writers are unable to complete projects because they lack a routine that nurtures the discipline of writing. Roy Peter Clark comments, "Most doctoral students who finish all their class work, and pass all examinations, and complete research for a dissertation never get a PhD. Why? Because they lack the simple discipline required to finish the writing."[15]

---

13. Roy Peter Clark details our tendencies: "Almost all writers procrastinate, so there's a good chance that you do too. Even among professionals, delay takes many forms." He goes on to list activities like checking emails, getting another cup of coffee, or staring into space. *Writing Tools: 55 Essential Strategies for Every Writer* (New York: Little, Brown, 2016), 200.

14. Currey, *Daily Rituals*, 145.

15. Clark, *Writing Tools*, 219. Often, the most difficult part of writing is getting started—typing the first word or sentence or paragraph. Gary Provost states,

So does this mean you should sit down at your computer (or your desk with paper and pen) and force yourself to write all day? What about taking breaks? Most people don't have the ability or focus to write for more than an hour at a time or cumulatively more than about three to four hours a day. That said, when it's time to write, all distractions (including responding to text messages and emails) need to be put aside and ignored.

DISTRACTING HABITS THAT HINDER WRITING

Explaining the why and how of undistracted work, Cal Newport defines "deep work" (a phrase he coined) as "professional activities performed in a state of distraction-free concentration that push your cognitive capabilities to their limit."[16] The idea is simple. In order to produce at our peak level, we need to work for extended periods with full concentration on a single task without interruption or distraction.[17]

Newport urges his readers not to confuse busyness with productivity. Checking and answering emails throughout the day, scheduling and attending meetings regularly, keeping up with social media, fitting in a load of laundry, roaming the halls to bounce ideas off those you encounter—these may make you *seem* busy, but they are often merely a parody of productivity. He admits that "to support deep work often requires the rejection of much of what is new and high tech."[18]

What makes deep work possible? Newport explains, "The key to developing a deep work habit is to move beyond good intentions and add *routine* and *rituals* to your working life designed to minimize the amount of your limited willpower necessary to transition into and maintain a state of unbroken concentration."[19] Indeed, distraction

---

"I love writing. It's getting started that I abhor." He suggests one way to avoid this trauma is to write in large blocks of time. *100 Ways to Improve Your Writing: Proven Professional Techniques for Writing with Style and Power*, updated ed. (New York: Berkley, 2019), 15.

16. Cal Newport, *Deep Work: Rules for Focused Success in a Distracted World* (New York: Grand Central, 2016), 3.

17. Newport, *Deep Work*, 44.

18. Newport, *Deep Work*, 69.

19. Newport, *Deep Work*, 100.

is a destroyer of depth.[20] Because writing takes great concentration, writers need to create environments where distractions are minimized and need to develop routines that foster productivity.[21]

AN EXAMPLE FROM THE ACADEMIC WORLD

As a junior faculty member, I (Adrianne) wasn't sure I'd ever find the time to write. Much of my time was focused on course development and teaching. In my first five years of teaching, I had only two semesters that did not include new course preparations, and a few of those semesters included two new course preparations. I found it next to impossible to block out time for writing during the regular semesters. Not only were my days filled with prep work and excruciatingly slow grading (I had not yet learned to grade at a quicker pace), but by the evenings I was exhausted. I lacked the mental energy to tackle writing. To be honest, I didn't really want to write in the evenings or on weekends. I wanted to spend time with my family, and I needed to spend time doing the things that did not get done during the week (e.g., laundry, grocery shopping, or house cleaning—all with the help of my husband and sons, but still time-consuming). In sum, my workload on the job and at home forced me to let go of the goal of writing regularly during the main semesters of my first few professional years. Instead, I dedicated my summers and breaks to intense writing.

The first summer of my professional career, I tried to adhere to a writing schedule but failed. I had planned to research and write Mondays through Thursdays in June and August. I had reserved July as my summer break because my children, who were year-round middle schoolers, would be on break that month. Somehow, June slipped through my fingers. Writing moved to the bottom of my to-do list as I read and prepared for a new course I was slated to teach in the fall. August ended before it began, and between a faculty workshop,

---

20. Newport, *Deep Work*, 134.

21. For practical advice on being more productive, see Tim Challies, *Do More Better: A Practical Guide to Productivity* (Minneapolis: Cruciform, 2015); and Matt Perman, *How to Get Unstuck: Breaking Free from Barriers to Your Productivity* (Grand Rapids: Zondervan, 2018).

meeting with new students, and being controlled by the tyranny of the urgent, I began the fall semester with no writing to show for that summer. My second summer, despite my renewed commitment to write, played out nearly identically to my first. But the third time was the charm! Throughout my third summer, I wrote. I began in late spring by writing and submitting an abstract to a professional conference. Once that paper was accepted, I had the outside pressure I needed to prioritize my writing. I allowed myself an hour or so each weekday morning to respond to emails or chat with colleagues; then I shut my office door (an important change from the previous summers) and worked on my conference paper, which I turned into a journal article the following summer.

These days, I still prefer to do the heavy lifting of research and writing in the summer months, and I continue to follow my Monday through Thursday work schedule. I have added writing times into my main semesters as well. I give myself some flexibility, but Thursdays and Fridays are my writing days. I allow myself to check emails in the mornings, but I ignore distractions and write or research until lunch. I check emails and texts, and then work without distractions until about five. Today is Thursday. There are four items on my to-do list, and I'm not sure what's for dinner tonight, but those things can wait. I am writing.

PRO TIPS FROM A SEASONED WRITER

Instead of providing a narrative of my writing schedule, I (Ben) will provide seven pro tips (or at least reflections) from my own experience.

1. *Everybody's writing schedule is different.* I realize that what I do is not what others do. I have friends who commit to a strict morning schedule of writing from, say, six to nine. I have not consistently kept such a schedule. There is no magic in having a particular schedule. We each have to discover (often by trial and error) a system that works best for us. Seek to gain wisdom and advice from others, but don't necessarily try to copy their routines. Come up with a routine that works for your family life, work schedule, personal preferences, and gifts.

2. *Life usually gets busier.* One of the things I've noticed is that life gets increasingly busier. The number of commitments I have now

compared to ten years ago has probably doubled. I find that the longer
I live somewhere, the busier I become as I say yes to more opportunities (related to family, church, school, etc.). This dilemma is mostly
my fault. I have agreed to take on most of these added responsibilities. If I don't make writing a priority in my life and build research
and writing into my schedule, my time will easily get swallowed up
by other important tasks.

3. *Write something every week*. It is probably not reasonable to say
most of us can or should attempt to write every day. A professional
writer's life revolves around their writing schedule. But for most
of us, who have full-time day jobs or are full-time students (often
with jobs as well), writing has to be done in the margins. And yet,
if we are not careful or intentional, weeks and months (and years!)
can go by without us making any significant progress on a project.
Then, finally, we give up altogether and become content with the
notion that we are just not good at writing. But by writing every
week (even if it is a small amount), we continue to make progress
and stay in the groove.

4. *Take advantage of breaks in your schedule*. Before our last week-
long midsemester break, I thought to myself that I could either write
all week or ride my motorcycle all week (always a tough decision for
me). Due to below-normal temperatures, I opted for the former. So
my plan for the week involved a three-pronged approach in divvy-
ing up my time: (1) mornings, record lectures for an online course;
(2) afternoons, research and write an essay; (3) evenings, read for a
new course development. Although this approach initially sounded
good, it was quickly abandoned. The first day I recorded lectures
in the morning and then transitioned to research and writing in the
afternoon. But, in order to maximize my undisturbed time that week,
I soon realized that the best use of my time would be to devote all
my time to task #2. Why? Because I knew tasks #1 and #3 wouldn't
require as much concentration and focus. Additionally, I know that it
can take hours of focused attention to be able to get the ball rolling
again on a project that has sat for a week or more. So, beginning on
Tuesday, I devoted all day (and a bit of the evening) to writing the
essay. The result was that by the end of the week I had produced a
ten-thousand-word essay, albeit in very rough condition. The other

projects that didn't get done are important to me, but I can easily work on them during the semester.

5. *Focus on one project at a time.* When I was in high school, I learned how to juggle. I can juggle three balls (or bean bags), including the cool trick of throwing one from behind my back. But when it comes to writing, it is best to focus on one project at a time (if possible) and not try to juggle work. Once I start a project, I like to attack it with all my energy until it is accomplished. Sometimes that is one week, and sometimes it is several years. Admittedly, several years ago I started a book and completed more than half of it and then had to lay it aside for about a year. Other projects took precedence and needed my immediate attention. That was hard for me and was not ideal. In the end, however, I was able to come back to the project and finish it (on time!).

6. *Know that different tasks in the writing process take different amounts of concentration.* Some tasks can be done in small blocks of time and don't require completely undisturbed attention (e.g., proofreading). But writing—actually putting words on a page—requires a significant amount of concentration and prolonged focus. Consequently, if I have a block of quiet, uninterrupted time, I make sure that I'm using that time to the fullest by not doing tasks that don't require as much focused effort.

7. *Get away in order to write.* I have found it a helpful practice to do writing retreats from time to time. These usually consist of two to four days of getting away by myself in order to write. No interruptions. No email. No errands. Just me, some books, and a computer. The amount I'm able to accomplish during these retreats would often take months in the throes of life's busyness.

CONCLUSION

We hope that it is clear to you at this point that to be an academic writer, you must put yourself in the habit of writing regularly. Perfect writing days seldom fall into your lap. Instead, you must build your writing habit. Find the time that works for you, make it a regular time, and commit yourself to the discipline of writing. Writing is a habit worth developing and worth protecting. Do not allow it to be usurped by checking emails or grading papers. Allow writing its own time and space because that is the only way progress will come. Copy the habits of successful writers and make writing a habit.

THE NEXT LEVEL

1. What are things in your day or week or month that keep you from being a productive writer?

_____

_____

_____

2. Can you envision a structured schedule that will provide you with at least several hours per week for research and writing? If so, what would that look like? For some people, three to four hours one day per week is sufficient. For others, one to two hours in the early morning (or late afternoon or nighttime) is best. The key is being consistent so that it becomes a habit.

_____

_____

_____

3. The tyranny of the urgent is real. In order to be a productive and consistent writer, you must protect your writing time and view it as urgent. On a scale of 1–10, how important is writing to you? Does your schedule reflect that importance? If not, make a commitment today to find a consistent time and place to write.

_____

_____

_____

7

Keep Writing,
Even after the First Draft

So many people think that once they have something down on paper, they're just about done. How many students finish a paper the night before it is due (or the morning it is due), print it out, and then turn it in? A paper is not finished after the first draft. That is merely the beginning of the editing process—similar to the selection of the ideal piece of wood before the carver begins to whittle away until the final image is clearly seen. William Zinsser reminds us that "professional writers rewrite their sentences over and over again and then rewrite what they have written."[1] Anne Huff comments, "New authors are often astounded by how many drafts lie behind a piece of work they admire. . . . Dozens of drafts are not unusual for considered scholarship."[2]

1. William Zinsser, *On Writing Well: The Classic Guide to Writing Nonfiction*, 7th ed., rev. and updated (New York: Harper Perennial, 2006), 4.
2. Anne Sigmund Huff, *Writing for Scholarly Publication* (Thousand Oaks, CA: Sage, 1999), 119. On a similar note, Anne Lamott says, "I know some very great writers, writers who you love who write beautifully and have made a great deal of money, and not *one* of them sits down routinely feeling wildly enthusiastic and confident. Not one of them writes elegant first drafts." *Bird by Bird: Some Instructions on Writing and Life*, 2nd ed. (New York: Anchor, 2019), 20–21.

Most people cannot write clearly, concisely, and convincingly in one draft. Ben usually proofreads his work at least ten times, and Adrianne loses count of how many times she proofreads. Patricia Goodson says, "Realistically, expect your first drafts always to be bad, even if you become a ridiculously productive writer. . . . If you want to write well, you must accept that you will be spending considerable time rewriting, rewriting, and rewriting some more. . . . By the time you finish writing and editing, you will have read through the text many, many times. It's not uncommon to do 20-plus rounds of editing, in some cases."[3] If twenty drafts seem overwhelming, take heart. Other writers suggest far fewer. For example, Eviatar Zerubavel encourages writers to work through four drafts,[4] and Melissa Donovan promotes a five-draft system.[5] We will discuss more about drafting below, but we must begin thinking about revising by thinking about rereading.

REREADING

The first step in editing is rereading what you have written, but we are not talking about a quick read-through. We are talking about slow, critical reading. This is the kind of effort Stephen King would call closed-door work. You want to be able to slowly read through the work without interruptions. Is it clear? Are you saying what you intended to say? Is your reasoning easy to follow, or do you find yourself needing to reread a phrase, a sentence, or a paragraph? Anything that causes you to reread or slow down is what Paula LaRocque calls a speedbump, and it likely needs reworking. She defines speedbumps as "errors in content or form. Distractions such as awkward phrasing. The wrong word. Dense, wordy, fuzzy, repetitive, tentative, or extraneous passages."[6] In order to read slowly and assume the persona of reader (as opposed to the writer who knows what he or she meant

---

3. Patricia Goodson, *Becoming an Academic Writer: 50 Exercises for Paced, Productive, and Powerful Writing*, 2nd ed. (Thousand Oaks, CA: Sage, 2017), xviii, 108, 138.

4. Eviatar Zerubavel, *The Clockwork Muse: A Practical Guide to Writing Theses, Dissertations, and Books* (Cambridge, MA: Harvard University Press, 1999), 49.

5. Melissa Donovan, *10 Core Practices for Better Writing* (San Francisco: Swan Hatch, 2013), 47–49.

6. Paula LaRocque, *The Book on Writing: The Ultimate Guide to Writing Well* (Arlington, TX: Grey & Guvnor, 2003), 174.

to say), it is often helpful to let a day or more pass after you finish your first draft before you pick it up to critically read it. In fact, if you can wait several days or a week, even better. If you reread soon after you finish writing, your brain will often make the text say what you want it to say, not what it actually says. We recommend this same waiting method when you reread each of your revisions. Time helps you forget at least some of the details of your writing, and familiarity is the enemy of editing.

After you let at least a day or two pass, you are ready to reread your draft. How should you read it? Should you print it out or read it on your screen? That is a question you will have to evaluate and answer for yourself. For me (Ben), it is always better to edit material when it is printed out—I see things differently when there is a hard copy. Huff says that she prefers paper to the computer because she "can see the whole so much more clearly."[7] You won't know until you try it both ways to see which works better for you. I (Adrianne) thought I edited my work pretty well on my screen. Then I printed it out and saw many things that I missed with on-screen editing.

We also encourage you to read your work aloud. Reading aloud forces you to slow down and read a bit more meticulously. You will hear awkward phrases more readily than you will see them. As LaRocque explains, reading aloud helps us find "hitches."[8] I (Adrianne) often encourage my writing students to edit their work aloud because when I am reading their papers I often think, "If she would have read this aloud, she would have recognized this problem and fixed it."

Another helpful editing technique is to read your work backwards. This would not be done on a first draft but on a polished draft. Read the last sentence first, then the one before it and so on. Reading backwards forces you to edit at the sentence level and can be an eye-opening approach to pruning your words.

REWRITING

Rereading leads to rewriting. As Donovan explains, "If you want to produce better writing (and become a better writer), then revisions

7. Huff, *Writing for Scholarly Publication*, 119.
8. LaRocque, *Book on Writing*, 174.

are absolutely essential."[9] We suggest you save each of your drafts as a
separate file. Do not simply write over your first draft in the same file
and save. Saving drafts in different files is a protection for the writer.
As you rewrite, you are continually thinking about your topic and
things that relate to it. Your thoughts and perspectives often change
and sharpen as you rewrite. What you might have cut out in a second
draft could end up being a crucial example in your fourth draft. It
is beyond discouraging to delete a sentence, paragraph, or section
and wish later that you still had it. Trying to rewrite that section is a
sad task, and we almost always think the unrecoverable original was
better. Similarly, you may find that your first draft includes too much
information and that you have two (or three) articles packed in that
single draft. Saving a copy of the rough draft and not editing that
file enables you to return to those thoughts later to develop another
writing project. You might choose to simply number your drafts and
save them as "first draft," "second draft," "third draft," and so on.
I (Adrianne) prefer labels that communicate a bit more about the
revision process. I save my files as "outline," "rough draft," "revised
draft," "reading draft," and "submission draft." I might have a couple
of revised drafts, which I will number. The reading draft is the draft
I give to others for feedback.

Your first draft is typically where you get all your thoughts organized on paper (or on the screen) as quickly and smoothly as possible. You do not want to slow down your train of thought, so you
should not get hung up on perfecting your sentences or other writing
details. Make a note of things you want to fix or double-check. I
(Adrianne) often turn the text of problem areas red, so I know to
focus on these areas during revisions and so I can free myself to move
forward with my argument while maintaining my train of thought.
Knowing that you will revise your work multiple times "helps relieve
much of the pressure as well as reduce much of the anxiety normally
involved in having to write it at all."[10] Get your first draft on paper;
then, as we said above, walk away from it for a time before you carefully reread it. Before making any changes during your rereading,

9. Donovan, *10 Core Practices*, 43.
10. Zerubavel, *Clockwork Muse*, 47.

save your file under another name (and do this for each additional reread and rewrite).

How many revisions should you do? That is up to you, but we suggest at least three closed-door revisions. The sweet spot may be around five drafts before asking a colleague to read and critique it (open-door revisions), but it depends on the kind of writer you are. You must find the number that works for you. Zerubavel encourages writers to "try to identify an optimal number that would not be too low, so as to allow yourself to take off some of the psychological pressure from each particular draft, yet at the same time also not too high, so as to avoid the risk of burnout."[11]

As you think about your number of revisions, think about your reader. First, think about the colleague who will be giving you feedback. You want to get your draft in the best shape you can before allowing another's eyes to critique it. How embarrassing to have your friend tell you they don't understand your argument or that you've used the wrong word here or misspelled something there. As you work through your drafts, "don't make any assumptions. If you're not sure about something, then look it up so you can fix a mistake (if there is one) and learn the correct way."[12] I (Adrianne) can't tell you how many times I've marked up student papers for mistakes that would have been so easy to look up and fix. Should the comma go before or after the quotation mark? Look it up. You don't have to memorize your style guide, but you do have to reference it often to make sure that you are doing things the correct way. We suggest revising until you cannot find a mistake, and that may take several printings, markups, and rewrites. Your edits will not end once you ask a colleague for feedback, but we will discuss that matter in chapters 8 and 9.

CUTTING

You reread and rewrite to make improvements, but often what makes a paper go from *good* to *great* is not what is added but what is cut.[13]

11. Zerubavel, *Clockwork Muse*, 49.
12. Donovan, *10 Core Practices*, 56.
13. Huff warns, "Don't fall in love with anything you have written. Be willing to cut, revise, and reorganize every word of every draft." *Writing for Scholarly Publication,*

But the task of cutting can be painful—like chopping off a limb from our own body. Our love for our work makes it difficult to cut unnecessary appendages. Roy Peter Clark warns, "When we fall in love with all our quotes, characters, anecdotes, and metaphors, we cannot bear to kill any of them. But kill we must."[14] "Kill the babies," LaRocque and others command, and be merciless.[15] It is a good skill to cut word count without cutting essential material. For example, instead of saying, "As a result of those things . . . ," write, "Consequently . . ." Less is almost always more (and better).

Consider these quotes from Zinsser in his classic work, *On Writing Well*:[16]

- "Writing improves in direct ratio to the number of things we can keep out of it that shouldn't be there."
- "Examine every word you put on paper. You'll find a surprising number that don't serve any purpose."
- "Most first drafts can be cut by 50 percent without losing any information or losing the author's voice."
- "Look for the clutter in your writing and prune it ruthlessly. Be grateful for everything you can throw away."
- "Writing is like a good watch—it should run smoothly and have no extra parts."

But what exactly should we cut? Here are a few suggestions:[17]

- Adverbs that intensify rather than modify: *just, certainly, entirely, extremely, completely, exactly.*

---

120. Stephen King uses the following formula: 2nd draft = 1st draft – 10 percent. *On Writing: A Memoir of the Craft* (New York: Scribner, 2000), 222.

14. Roy Peter Clark, *Writing Tools: 55 Essential Strategies for Every Writer* (New York: Little, Brown, 2016), 50. He later says, "Quality comes from revision" (203).

15. LaRocque, *Book on Writing*, 79.

16. Zinsser, *On Writing Well*, 12, 16, 84. This sentiment is common among writers and editors. For example, William Strunk and E. B. White claim, "Vigorous writing is concise." *The Elements of Style*, 4th ed. (Boston: Pearson, 2000), 23. Likewise, Gary Provost claims that "shorter is almost always better." *100 Ways to Improve Your Writing: Proven Professional Techniques for Writing with Style and Power* (New York: Berkley, 2019), 62.

17. The following suggestions of what to cut are based on Clark, *Writing Tools*, 52.

- Prepositional phrases that repeat the obvious: *in the story*, *in the article*, *in the movie*, *in the city*.
- Phrases that grow on verbs: *seems to*, *tends to*, *should have to*, *tries to*.
- Abstract nouns that hide active verbs: *consideration* becomes *considers*; *judgment* becomes *judges*; *observation* becomes *observes*.
- Redundancy: *a sultry, humid afternoon*.

Cutting sharpens the focus of your manuscript (and you have saved what you cut in a previous draft file for possible future use). Cutting, tweaking, and streamlining are vital methods for improving the final product. This truth about the writing process also means that you must give yourself enough time to properly edit and revise your work.[18]

BENEFITS OF REWRITING

As you take (or redeem) the time to revise your writing in multiple drafts, you will discover your own writing weaknesses.[19] Do you love adverbs more than you should? Do you have a propensity to *tell* instead of *show*? In other words, are you writing, "It is interesting to note . . . ," or are your sentences and content producing interest in your reader? Your revisions will show you your writing faults, and knowing them will enable you in future first drafts to begin to overcome these tendencies. Thus, revising not only improves your manuscript, but it also makes you a better writer. Embrace the process of revision. Allow it to take some pressure off you during your early drafts. Give yourself a long runway on your writing schedule so that you can work through multiple drafts. Enjoy developing your thinking through writing and revising. Embrace this aspect of becoming a better writer. As Donovan explains, "If you don't take time to polish your writing, why should anyone make time to read it?"[20]

18. Many students do not edit and revise their work simply because they didn't budget time for it. Clark writes, "The wise student starts 'writing' the paper the day it is assigned." *Writing Tools*, 201.
19. Donovan, *10 Core Practices*, 44.
20. Donovan, *10 Core Practices*, 50.

CONCLUSION

Writing is a process, one that doesn't end with the sigh of relief that comes after you finish your first draft. You must reread that draft so that you can improve it. Like a good sauce, a manuscript needs to simmer for a bit. It needs to be retasted and its seasonings adjusted to become excellent. Your "reseasoning" will include some removing and reworking. As we noted above, do not be afraid to cut and clarify. Good writing cannot be a clutter of words, ideas, or examples. Rather, it is made up of words, ideas, and examples in sharp focus. Embrace the editing process and become a critical reader of your own work, a fearless editor, and a better writer through it all.

THE NEXT LEVEL

1. Print out the first two pages of your current writing project (or any two pages that are in a decent first draft state). Before reading the printed pages, carefully read the two pages on the screen and highlight any typos or speedbumps you find. Then read the printed pages highlighting typos and speedbumps. In which format were you able to find more mistakes? This is a small test but could help you determine which format works best for you.

2. Look at your schedule for your current article or class-paper-length writing project. Working backward from the due date, set your rough (or first) draft to be due two weeks before that due date. And schedule at least three closed-door readings and revisions before submitting your paper. If your official due date is the fourteenth of the month, your revised due date is the first. Your closed-door reading day is the fifth. Make the revisions on the sixth or seventh. Carefully reread your revised draft on the tenth. Make revisions on the tenth or eleventh. Carefully reread your revised draft on the twelfth and revise again before submitting it on the fourteenth. (If you'd like a colleague to read your paper and give you feedback, add in an additional buffer of at least a week. Do all your revisions, then give your colleague a week to provide you feedback.)

3. Carefully read your most recent manuscript draft with an eye toward cutting unnecessary words, sentences, or paragraphs. Circle or highlight intensifying adverbs, prepositional phrases that repeat the obvious, phrases that grow on verbs, abstract nouns, redundancy, and so on. Of the items circled or high-lighted, what can you cut or reword for concision and sharper focus?

8

Solicit Feedback

Not only must you give yourself ample time to proofread your work; you must also allow for other people to review your work. Most authors cannot properly or completely edit their own writing. After a while you become blinded to your own mistakes and unhealthy patterns. You fill in missing words because you know what you intended to say. You rationalize the use of adverbs that are *completely* and *utterly* unnecessary. You tend to allow for words that *seem to* grow on verbs. You offer *justification* for nouns of abstraction. And you don't mind when you *restate* ideas with words or phrases you have already used.

We are bad self-critics. Oh, give me (Ben) someone else's work, and I'll destroy it as I wield my red pen like a Spanish swordsman. I will vanquish my foe (bad grammar) with a slash here and a squiggle there, until it yields, pleading for mercy. But as soon as I see my own work, my skill at hunting down bad grammar diminishes, and I can greatly benefit from the help of others. Because we struggle as self-critics, even after we have reread, reviewed, and turned our work into a polished draft, we must unlock our closed door and invite some open-door critiquing.

DIFFERENT READERS, DIFFERENT PERSPECTIVES

The general principle that I (Ben) follow is this: the more eyes I can get on my writing, the better.[1] I am currently the editor of *Southeastern*

---

1. Anne Lamott states, "I always show my work to one or two people before sending a copy to my editor or agent." *Bird by Bird: Some Instructions on Writing and Life*, 2nd ed. (New York: Anchor, 2019), 153.

Theological Review, a double-blind, peer-reviewed journal. Every essay that is accepted for publication is read and edited by a minimum of five people (besides the author and those who read the essay before I received it). First, I send the essay to two referees who read mainly for content and secondarily for form and style. It is then edited by me and two assistants who carefully read the work. Each person who edits the work finds mistakes. I am certain that if I had additional help, others could also make recommendations to improve the piece before it is published. At some point, however, you have to fight off your perfectionist tendencies (if you have them) and publish the work. My editorial work proves my point—the more eyes the better—because each set of eyes improves the work in ways that other eyes have missed.

Each person who reads your work will bring a different perspective and different skills to bear on your text and will find things that others did not see. Recruit people who are good at English and grammar and who are willing to read your work. Also, find people with different skills: (1) theologians or specialists in your area, (2) English majors, and (3) individuals not trained at seminaries or graduate schools (or those with other occupations such as engineers, nurses, stay-at-home moms, etc.).

WHOM TO ASK

It is helpful to have a strategy for getting others to proofread your work. We propose a three-level progressive method:[2]

- *Early drafts: nonexperts.* Nonexperts can be defined as those who "do not hold a terminal degree in your field, and they are 'people you have absolutely no need to impress.'"[3]
- *Middle drafts: peer review.* For faculty this might be a graduate student or an assistant. For a student this might be another

2. This three-level method of progressive proofreading is summarized from Patricia Goodson, *Becoming an Academic Writer: 50 Exercises for Paced, Productive, and Powerful Writing*, 2nd ed. (Thousand Oaks, CA: Sage, 2017), 92–99.

3. Goodson, *Becoming an Academic Writer*, 92, citing Tara Grey, *Publish and Flourish* (Springfield, IL: Teaching Academy, New Mexico State University, 2005), 57.

student. These types of readers are best "at anticipating questions and quick at catching unclear wording."[4]

- *Final drafts: expert review.* Experts "include your dissertation or thesis advisors, committee members, or faculty colleagues."[5]

These types of reviewers bring different perspectives to your work and different benefits. For example, because nonexperts need clear explanations, detailed examples, and simple definitions, your nonexpert reviewers will require you to communicate with extreme clarity and without making assumptions. The goal at this stage is to gain feedback that "provides input regarding *what* is being said—and how it impacts the reader."[6]

Finding a nonexpert reviewer can be more challenging than one might think. You could start by considering the people you live with or have lived with, like your mother, father, sibling, or spouse. However, you must critically evaluate the quality of the criticism you will get from a person who loves you. If your mom is only going to tell you how great your work is, she is a wonderful cheerleader but not a helpful reviewer because her reading will not lead to improvements in your text. Some moms and other family members are excellent nonexpert reviewers; some are not. Test them out to determine whether they can be objective and helpfully critical. You might also consider asking a friend who is not in your field of research, perhaps a friend from church or a coworker if you hold a nonacademic job.

If your school has a writing center, we suggest you take your early draft there. The consultants there are not likely to be experts in your field (unless your field is composition). They are also not likely to be your friends or your family, so they are in a good position to be objective and helpful. We have found that the writing center on our campus is an excellent, free, and ridiculously underused resource. If you have access to such a resource, please take advantage of it.

4. Goodson, *Becoming an Academic Writer*, 95. She explains: "If you are a student, your peers are the kind of readers who know just enough about the topic to anticipate the questions other readers might ask; they know enough to be able to identify the places where the text could be clearer and point out instances where the text flow breaks down."

5. Goodson, *Becoming an Academic Writer*, 97.

6. Goodson, *Becoming an Academic Writer*, 95.

After you address the comments and suggestions from your nonexpert reviewers, you'll want a peer or two to read your updated draft. The goal of a peer review is to gain criterion-based feedback that provides "input regarding *how* you're saying [what you are saying]—as well as what needs to change to improve communication."[7] If you are a student, critically consider the other students in your classes. Who seems to be prepared to engage in thoughtful discussion in the classroom? Who likes to hear themselves talk? Avoid the constant talkers and approach the thoughtful discussers. If you are part of an academic cohort, ask a peer in your cohort to read your paper. When you ask, it is polite to offer to read and give feedback on their work as well. By initiating these types of symbiotic academic relationships, you will not only improve your writing in the present, but you will also be cultivating professional relationships that could help you down the line as your cohort goes on to become faculty members at various institutions in the future. Students working on class papers may stop with this round of review, but students writing theses or dissertations will want and need final draft reviews as well.

If you are a faculty member, this middle draft is the one to give to your graduate assistant or researcher. Not only will they give you helpful feedback (if you make it clear that they may and should do that), but this is also a helpful opportunity to teach them about the process of revisions needed to improve academic work. You might also ask a junior faculty member to review your work, but be careful not to add work for an already overloaded individual. Make it clear that the graduate student or the junior faculty member may decline your request. Depending on your situation, you might ask your secretary to read this draft. I (Adrianne) have been blessed with one of the best proofreading secretaries around. She catches so many of my typos and tells me what does not make sense in my arguments and what is unclear in my discussion. Not all secretaries are great proofreaders, but many are. And the ones who have worked in your department for several years are often familiar enough with your field to help you improve the content and style of your manuscript.

7. Goodson, *Becoming an Academic Writer*, 95.

After editing your draft according to the suggestions of your middle draft reviewers, it is time to pass your new version off for a final review by an expert in your field before submitting your work for publication.[8] With expert reviewers, you are after content-related feedback since they are competent to evaluate the quality of your writing as well as the value of your ideas. They can also determine how your ideas fit within the current dialogue in the field. Goodson says, "Their input is the last thing you add to make your piece picture-perfect!"[9] Students should ask their thesis or dissertation advisers to read this draft. They will also ask their thesis or dissertation committee members to read a draft before their defense, but not this draft. It is best to have your adviser read a first final draft, so that you can address his or her comments before sending an improved draft to committee members for feedback prior to your defense.

A faculty member should ask another faculty member in his or her field to offer feedback on this draft. If you are new to your institution, you may feel uncomfortable asking a colleague for critique, but this can be a great way to begin a good working relationship or even friendship. You might also consider a colleague from graduate school who is a faculty member at another institution. We will talk more about conferences in chapter 10, but colleagues who are interested in your presentation at a conference can become great resources for reviewing your paper.

HOW TO ASK

When approaching someone to review your work, regardless of whether you are at the early, middle, or final draft stage, keep in mind that they are doing a favor for you. Therefore, you want to make their work as easy as possible for them. Give them the cleanest draft

---

8. Although we are using the term *final draft* to distinguish this draft from the early and middle drafts, this draft is not anyone's final draft. After the expert reviewers make their notes, you will revise your manuscript for submission. If your submission is accepted for publication, the editors may ask for a few more drafts before you arrive at the draft that will be published.

9. Goodson, *Becoming an Academic Writer*, 97.

you can. Discuss a timeline that works for both of you. You might prefer to have the review back in a week, but your friend could have a big work deadline that week. Be respectful of their commitments and work out a timeline that works for you both. Set a deadline for the review that you both agree on. This alleviates awkwardness when you see one another on campus, at church, or in the neighborhood and helps you refrain from inundating your reviewer with emails about his or her progress. Offer to review your reviewer's work in the future and be sure to thank them afterward. For colleagues who trade drafts for review with you, a simple thank-you is likely sufficient, but for those who have no drafts to give you (e.g., your mom, a nonacademic coworker, friend, secretary), it might be nice to buy them a cup of coffee or a cheeseburger as a sign of your appreciation. We also encourage you to publicly thank your reviewers in the acknowledgments section of your published work.

Once you have your reviewer's comments in hand, avoid reading those comments in front of your reviewer. Some comments may come across as harsh, and there may be other comments that you disagree with.[10] It is best to read the comments in private and not react immediately. Read them and let them sit at least overnight before reading them again. Try to read them objectively, keeping in mind that your reviewer is trying to improve your paper. Often a first reading of comments can be a hit to the ego; but after they sit and you read them again, you tend to see the wisdom in the suggestions. If you have questions about any comments, ask the reviewer for clarifications, but do not defend aspects of your paper they questioned or criticized. Work to clarify those sections or add explanations for why they are an integral part of your argument. It is better to hear these critiques from a friend or peer than from a publisher who is rejecting your work.

At any point in your revising process, someone you ask to read your draft might decline your request. What should you do if someone says no to you? Be gracious. Be polite. Remember that you are asking for a big favor that takes up a decent amount of a person's time. Carefully reading and commenting on an article-length paper

---

10. We discuss dealing with critical feedback in more detail in chapter 9.

may take two to four hours. Giving critical attention to a thesis, dissertation, or book manuscript will take several days. If a potential reviewer declines, thank them for considering your request. Do not make them feel guilty for saying no. You might even offer to read their work in the future as an indication of goodwill. You too may have to say no to a request like this sometimes because you are stretched too thin and cannot give it the attention it deserves. Be as gracious to your potential reviewer as you would want them to be to you if the roles were reversed.

WRITING COMMUNITIES

Many books on writing encourage participation in some sort of writing community,[11] and we would be remiss not to point out the feedback benefits of doing so, whether by joining a regularly meeting writing group, going on periodic writing retreats, or connecting with an online writing network. A regular meeting group (in person or online) is most beneficial to regular writers—and in earlier chapters we have stressed the importance of writing regularly. Such groups can be as small as two to three people who support one another's writing goals. Helen Sword emphasizes that "*support* is crucial," and she explains that "a genuinely supportive writing group demonstrates a collective concern for the growth, development, and well-being of every member."[12] If your department or school has a writing group, we encourage you to try it out.[13] If there is not a writing group for you to join, start one. Rowena Murray lays out a plan for starting a writing group in her book *Writing for Academic Journals*.[14] Within

11. See, e.g., Melissa Donovan, *10 Core Practices for Better Writing* (San Francisco: Swan Hatch, 2013), 163–266; Rowena Murray, *Writing for Academic Journals*, 4th ed. (London: Open University Press, 2020), 157–73; and Helen Sword, *Air & Light & Time & Space: How Successful Academics Write* (Cambridge, MA: Harvard University Press, 2017), 135–51.

12. Sword, *Air & Light & Time & Space*, 138.

13. Not only are writing groups great places to receive helpful feedback, but they also encourage regular writing times. They are more difficult to blow off than your own closed-door writing sessions and have proved beneficial to many writers across all disciplines.

14. Murray, *Writing for Academic Journals*, 158–63.

such a group, there is time for quietly writing in the company of other writers, time for discussing your work and ideas, and time for providing one another with critical feedback. Because everyone present is there to improve their writing, giving and receiving feedback is part of the group's purpose. Thus, you have a network of reviewers that you are not imposing on because you also serve as their reviewer.

If you are a writer who is unable to write regularly during the year, a writing retreat could be just what you need. Your school or department may have funds to support a writing retreat as part of its faculty development initiative, and you could step up and organize a weekend away for writing. You could also search online for an appropriate writing retreat to attend. Research shows that writing retreats "appear to be especially powerful for academic women, who, if statistics reported in the literature are anything to go by, are attracted to communal professional-development events in significantly greater numbers than men."[15] Regardless of the type of writing community, your participation will help you advance your writing as you work with like-minded individuals.

CONCLUSION

However you solicit and receive feedback on your writing—whether it is through writing communities or from friends, colleagues, students, or advisers—the main goal is to allow others to see what you cannot see because you are too close to your own writing. You want them to find the holes in your arguments and the problems with your word choices and punctuation, and you need this because we are all bad self-critics. We need many eyes on our projects—the more the better. Different eyes bring different perspectives, and we need different kinds of reviewers (academic and nonacademic) to help us communicate our thoughts clearly and concisely. We need feedback, both the feedback that makes us smile and the feedback that makes us cringe (and sometimes cry). As Melissa Donovan explains, "Those early, private critiques give us a chance to improve our work, so hopefully

15. Sword, *Air & Light & Time & Space*, 141–42.

the later, more public reviews won't be so difficult to deal with."[16] In sum, "when approached thoughtfully, critiques do far more good for your writing than harm."[17]

THE NEXT LEVEL

1. Who are some nonexperts whom you could ask to read an early draft of your manuscript? Try to come up with four or five names of potential readers, then rank them according to whom you would like to ask first.

    1. _____

    2. _____

    3. _____

    4. _____

    5. _____

2. Who are some peers whom you could ask to read a middle draft of your manuscript? Try to come up with three or four names of potential readers, then rank them according to whom you would like to ask first.

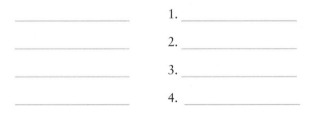

    1. _____

    2. _____

    3. _____

    4. _____

16. Donovan, *10 Core Practices*, 122.
17. Donovan, *10 Core Practices*, 105.

3. Who are some experts whom you could ask to read a final draft of your manuscript? Try to come up with two or three names of potential readers, then rank them according to whom you would like to ask first.

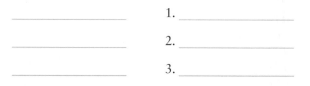

    1. _____

    2. _____

    3. _____

4. Would you like to start a writing community? If so, reach out to some of the people in the lists above and invite them to help you. The "Writing Group Starter Kit," an online resource from the University of North Carolina at Chapel Hill's Writing Center, may be helpful.[18] (We told you that writing centers are underutilized!)

5. When is the deadline for your current writing project? Work backward on the calendar to create the deadline for your early draft (a draft as polished as you can make it behind your closed door), leaving enough time for a nonexpert to review it and for you to revise it, give it to a peer for review, revise it again, give it to an expert, and revise it again before the actual deadline.

Actual deadline: _____

Deadline for expert reviewer's review: _____

Deadline to give final draft to expert reviewer: _____

Deadline for peer reviewer's review: _____

Deadline to give middle draft to peer reviewer: _____

Deadline for nonexpert reviewer's review: _____

Deadline to give early draft to nonexpert reviewer: _____

18. "Writing Group Starter Kit," The Writing Center, University of North Carolina at Chapel Hill (2022), https://writingcenter.unc.edu/tips-and-tools/writing-groups/writing-group-starter-kit/?msclkid=f6e46637c5a611ecb6fc037ce525358c.

Remember to give yourself enough time to polish your early draft with closed-door careful rereadings and revisions as discussed in the previous chapter. Good papers take time. Great papers take more time, but it is time well spent because the rewards of this time-consuming process pay off in the quality of the final product.

6. How will you thank your reviewers?

_____

_____

_____

9

Don't Be Afraid of Feedback

Nearly everybody, including the most prolific authors, has had their work rejected by editors or publishers. Allow us to offer two examples of well-known authors who faced rejection early in their careers. The first is John Grisham. As a newly minted lawyer, Grisham began writing while working sixty to eighty hours a week. He got up at five every morning and worked on his amateurish writing for at least one hour before attending to his official business. After three long years of hard work, his first novel, *A Time to Kill*, was finally completed in 1987. He was rejected by twenty-eight publishers before signing a contract. The book company printed only five thousand copies of the novel and gave him a $15,000 advance. It wasn't until his second volume, *The Firm*, that he got his big break. Paramount Pictures paid him $600,000 for the rights to make the plot into a movie. Now, virtually every book Grisham writes is a bestseller.[1]

The other example is that of J. K. Rowling. In 1995, Rowling finished her manuscript for *Harry Potter and the Philosopher's Stone*, which was typed on an old manual typewriter. After she acquired an agent, the book was submitted to twelve publishing houses, all of which rejected the manuscript. A year later she was finally given

1. Wikipedia, s.v. "John Grisham," last modified January 2, 2023, https://en.wikipedia.org/wiki/John_Grisham.

the green light (and a £1,500 advance) by Bloomsbury, a publishing house in London. Although Bloomsbury agreed to publish the book, they advised Rowling to get a day job, since she had little chance of making money in children's books. In June 1997, Bloomsbury published *Philosopher's Stone* with an initial print run of five hundred copies. At the time of this writing, such copies are valued between £16,000 and £25,000. Five months later, the book won its first award (at least two others followed). Scholastic bought the rights to publish the book for $105,000. Rowling said that she "nearly died" when she heard the news.[2]

Fast-forward to 2007 and the release of the seventh book in the series, *Harry Potter and the Deathly Hallows*. It holds the record as the fastest-selling book of all time (eleven million copies sold on the first day of its release). The series has now sold more than five hundred million copies and has been translated into more than eighty languages, making it the best-selling series in history. *Harry Potter* is now a global brand worth an estimated $25 billion (in 2016).[3] In 2004, Forbes named Rowling as the first person to become a US-dollar billionaire by writing books.[4]

There are other famous authors whose work was initially rejected that we could mention as well: Dr. Seuss, Agatha Christie, and Stephen King. Indeed, on a much smaller scale, I (Ben) can relate to these authors; my first book was rejected by nearly a dozen publishers. My point is that rejection is common, and you should not give up simply because one or two or twelve publishers reject your work.

Rejection is not limited to book publishers. When it comes to academic journals, just assume that it will take two or three journals before you find a home for your work.[5] The better journals will

2. "J. K. Rowling Biography: Success Story of the 'Harry Potter' Author," Astrum People (website), accessed January 23, 2023, https://astrumpeople.com/jk-rowling.

3. Katie Mayer, "Harry Potter's $25 Billion Magic Spell," *Money*, April 6, 2016, https://money.com/billion-dollar-spell-harry-potter.

4. Julie Watson and Tomas Kellner, "J. K. Rowling and the Billion-Dollar Empire," *Forbes*, February 26, 2004, www.forbes.com/maserati/billionaires2004/cx_jw_0226rowlingbill04.html.

5. Nancy Jean Vyhmeister notes, "New writers can expect rejection letters. Please don't be upset if that happens to you! Take any and all instructions into consideration and write your article over." *Your Guide to Writing Quality Research Papers: For Students of Religion and Theology* (Grand Rapids: Zondervan, 2014), 73.

tell you why your essay was rejected. As the editor of *Southeastern Theological Review*, I (Ben) pay two experts to read and evaluate the essays that I receive. If an essay is rejected, I pass on the feedback to the author, who can then incorporate those comments to improve the essay for the next journal. Jensen reminds us that "the review process is not designed to be warm and fuzzy."[6] It is humbling to receive critical feedback. But we must take such comments as opportunities to improve our work. Yes, you will get rejected. We all do. Some suggest that you should not give up on publishing a journal article until it has been rejected three times.[7] Don't give up. Keep trying until your work is published.[8]

CRITICISM AND EGOS

Writing and publishing are not unlike parenting in some ways. Writers often refer to their works as their babies. I (Adrianne) am reminded of a stark realization I had at a parenting conference years ago. The speaker welcomed all of us eager-to-learn parents and then slapped us with an ugly truth. He said most parents don't really want to learn to be better parents; they just want perfect kids. When it comes to writing, most writers don't want to be told how they can improve their writing, they just want perfect books, articles, or blogs. Neither writing nor parenting works this way. We make mistakes. We are not as clear as we thought we were. We need another set of eyes to help us improve, and that is what critical feedback is—an avenue for improvement.

Sometimes, however, feedback can feel more like a path to pain than an avenue for improvement. Remember that a critique of your work is not a personal attack. Remind yourself to be grateful that the reviewer thought your paper was worthy of critique. And most

6. Joli Jensen, *Write No Matter What: Advice for Academics* (Chicago: University of Chicago Press, 2017), 60.

7. Gary J. Skolits, Ralph G. Brockett, and Roger Hiemstra, "Publishing in Peer-Reviewed and Nonreviewed Journals," in *The Handbook of Scholarly Writing and Publishing*, ed. Tonette S. Rocco and Tim Hatcher (San Francisco: Jossey-Bass, 2011), 24.

8. For helpful suggestions on writing proposals, see Susan Rabiner and Alfred Fortunato, *Thinking like Your Editor: How to Write Great Serious Nonfiction and Get It Published* (New York: Norton, 2002).

importantly, put your ego in the closet and lock the door! Writers, like athletes, are always in training. A reviewer telling a writer to clarify her focus should not be a threat to the writer's self-worth any more than a tennis coach telling a player to work on her backhand. Tennis players who want to keep playing tennis will accept coaching as they work to improve their game. Likewise, writers who want to keep writing must learn to receive feedback as coaching that can be used to improve their writing.

IT'S NOT A PERSONAL INSULT

Not all reviewers come across as kind. Some are both helpful and encouraging, like those who handwrote notes on some of Stephen King's rejection letters. One said, "This is good. Not for us, but good. You have talent. Submit again."[9] Other reviews, while helpful in the long run, may come across as discouraging in the moment. Some rejections seem encouraging on the surface, such as when an editor says they are sorry that your article has not been recommended for publication by the reviewers but that they hope the enclosed evaluations will be useful in revising. Sometimes editors will even encourage writers to send them other essays in the future. However, harsher comments can make the writer feel angry and hurt. Comments that the writing is littered with vague or meaningless statements are tough criticisms to digest. Often reviewers use phrases that seem more evaluative than objective. Reviewers might also come across as snide when their comments appear more sarcastic than instructive. Reading harsh reviews can feel like jabs of a stiletto in the gut and cause the writer to feel hurt, angry, and embarrassed. When this happens, walk away for a bit. Hide the review in a drawer for a few weeks, then toughen up your skin and take advantage of the help it offers.

I (Adrianne) am reminded of a former student of mine who told me that my comments on her paper made her cry. What? I was shocked and saddened. I never meant to make anyone cry. My comments were intended to help students improve their work. Admittedly, when I am tired or nearing the bottom of a stack of grading, I'm less congenial

9. Stephen King, *On Writing: A Memoir of the Craft* (New York: Scribner, 2000), 41.

in my comments and more to the point. At those times, my need for speed (so I can hurry up and finish) overcomes my self-awareness of politeness. Perhaps the reviewers who hurt our egos were also tired when they read our manuscripts. Perhaps your submission was the last paper in a stack of papers, and the reviewer had used up all her congeniality for the day. Or maybe she is simply a straightforward, just-the-facts kind of reviewer. Regardless, we need to set aside our egos and work through the comments. Most criticisms (even the harsh ones) are valid, and as we address them our writing improves significantly.

DIGESTING FEEDBACK

If you have solicited feedback from a nonexpert, peer, or expert reviewer, make it clear what you want from them when you give them your manuscript. Brandon J. O'Brien lists some helpful criteria:

1. What am I doing well? What is helpful or insightful about my work?
2. Be honest. Point out areas that are unclear, redundant, or inaccurate.
3. Be as specific as possible in praise and critique (so that I can improve the work in specific ways).
4. Offer specific revisions if and when you can.[10]

As you read through the feedback, assume the reviewer did what you asked to the best of their abilities. Be grateful for the feedback and take every note into consideration. Writers are often tempted to dismiss comments with which they don't agree. Don't do that. Instead, add a sentence noting your counterpoint and explaining why the position offered as criticism doesn't apply in this situation. Future readers are likely to have the same issue or question. It is in your best interest as a writer to address the critiques before publication, thus saving yourself potential public embarrassment in a published book review or rebuttal to your article.

10. Summarized from Brandon J. O'Brien, *Writing for Life and Ministry* (Chicago: Moody, 2020), 111.

Use the feedback to improve your paper, but do not let the feedback have more power over you than it should. As Melissa Donovan notes, it is normal to have an emotional reaction to a critique of your work.[11] As we said before, your work can feel like your baby, and it can hurt to discover that your baby isn't perfect. Because of the potential for an emotional response, "do not review the critique in the presence of the person who prepared it."[12] Find a private place to read through the comments; then let them sit for a few days; "in time, your emotions will subside and your intellect will take over."[13] If you reread the comments and still feel hurt or angry, let it sit a bit longer. Eventually, you will be able to read them without cringing, and then you can get to work.

Some critiques can be particularly harsh and difficult to process. Donovan provides the following helpful tips for dealing with those hurtful critiques.[14]

- Tell your ego to take a nap.
- Detach emotionally.
- You are not your writing.
- You're only human. Nobody's perfect.
- Put it aside.
- Look for the good.
- Find the subjective.
- Get a second opinion.
- Devise a plan for applying the feedback to your work.
- Improve your work.

Donovan's final bulleted point is key; we digest the critiques of others so that we can improve our work. The improvement from my (Adrianne's) prereview article to the postreview article turned out to make the difference between rejection and acceptance for publication.

---

11. Melissa Donovan, *10 Core Practices for Better Writing* (San Francisco: Swan Hatch, 2013), 109.
12. Donovan, *10 Core Practices*, 109.
13. Donovan, *10 Core Practices*, 109.
14. Donovan, *10 Core Practices*, 112–15.

After I addressed the comments from the reviewers and resubmitted my article, it was accepted without any required revisions. Despite the pain of those comments, they helped me get what I wanted—an improved paper that was accepted for publication.

PROVIDING FEEDBACK

Working through the feedback we receive on our writing can (and should) make us better at providing feedback for others. Providing feedback is an opportunity to help a fellow scholar. Whether you are being paid to review works or not, whether you are reviewing for a friend, a colleague, or a student, carve out enough time to give each work your undivided attention and your best critical eye. I (Adrianne) require peer review work in my writing classes because reviewing is part of the writing world. If student writers do not learn how to be helpful reviewers in the classroom or through books like this one, they may be tempted to think that reviewers are supposed to be harsh critics. However, the best reviewers are the ones who demonstrate neighbor love through their comments.

Neighbor love is one of the most important aspects of review work. The Bible tells us that we should behave toward our neighbors as we would want them to behave toward us (Matt. 7:12) and that loving our neighbor as we love ourselves is the second-greatest commandment (Mark 12:31). Think about your own writing. Think about the care you put into your work. Strive to review another's work with that same kind of care. As you review, think about how you word your comments. Your feedback should encourage improvements, not induce discouragement. To love your neighbor well, you must point out flaws or weaknesses in their work, but you can do this with grace. It is the opposite of loving to say that "everything looks good" when it doesn't, which then might pave the way for more public criticism in the future.

As we mentioned above, carve out enough time to review a work well. If you are a paid reviewer, you will have to meet the publisher's timeline, but you are not without a voice. If you cannot complete a review in the given time, be honest with the publisher and work to renegotiate the timeline or review another piece with a deadline further out. If you are reviewing for a colleague or student, be honest about how soon you can get your notes back to them and stick to your promise. If you become delayed, reach out to the writer to let him or her know what is going on. Honesty about your time management will help the writer fight against the urge to nag you for your feedback.

You not only need the time to review; you also need a place to review. That place should not be in the presence of the writer. You need a quiet, private space where you can read the work without feeling any pressure from the writer (or anyone else).

Give yourself time to read the work more than once. Read it the first time to get a sense of the argument and the direction of the work. For a short piece, like a journal article, complete the first read-through in one sitting. For a longer work, like a monograph, complete your first read-through as quickly as possible so that you can understand the trajectory and hold the internal connections in your mind as you read. You might finish your first read-through in a couple of days. Strive to finish within a week.

After you've read through the piece once, reread with your pen or highlighter and take notes as you go. Look for and highlight the strengths of the work. You want to be able to encourage the writer with the things he or she is doing well. If an example is particularly illuminating in the discussion, note that. If a connection or application is compelling, point that out to the writer. Exercise neighbor love by pointing out the things the writer is doing well. Also note areas that need to be clarified. If sections, paragraphs, or sentences slowed you down as you read, figure out why they slowed you down and include that information in your comments.

Once you've marked up the work and made your notes, you must organize your thoughts and prepare your critique.[15] Do not give the writer your raw notes. Those are for your eyes only and may come across as hurtful or insensitive to the writer. Instead, prepare an organized report of your feedback. Begin with what the writer did well. In other words, "kick off the critique on a positive note."[16] Beginning with the good helps to establish you as a helpful reviewer

15. Donovan, *10 Core Practices*, 118.
16. Donovan, *10 Core Practices*, 118.

in the writer's eyes. When the writer sees that there are elements of her work that you appreciate, she will be more open to the negative feedback meant to help her improve.

When you get to the areas for improvement, try to use positive language and avoid negative words or evaluative words disguised as descriptors, and do not criticize the writer.[17] Using positive language and avoiding negative words are two sides of the same coin. Instead of saying an argument is weak or an example is unhelpful, "tell the writer what actions they can take to make it better."[18] Perhaps they might strengthen the argument by narrowing the focus. Perhaps an example that connects the minor argument with the main argument would add strength. Edit out evaluative language meant to be descriptive. Instead of saying something like, "Useless adverbs *litter* the manuscript," say, "Delete unnecessary adverbs throughout." This kind of feedback will take longer to provide and require more work on your part, but it will be more beneficial to the writer. This is the kind of feedback we all want, so it is the kind of feedback we should all give as we remember that reviewing is an exercise in neighbor love.

As reviewers, we can help writers keep from wrapping their identity or self-worth into their writing by using text-oriented, as opposed to writer-oriented, language. Edit "you" and "your" out of your critical review. Instead of saying "you aren't clear" or "your wording isn't clear," focus on the text and say, "This paragraph or sentence is unclear." Donovan reminds us to "keep the work and the writer separate and only critique the work."[19]

Once your feedback report is ready, let it sit for a day (if the timeline allows) so that you can proofread it again for clarity and kindness. Also proofread your markups on your copy of the text. Reword anything that focuses on the writer rather than the written text and replace negative language with positive language. If you are reviewing for a publisher, your work is done once you submit this information. If you are reviewing for a colleague or student, however, consider going the extra mile and offering to discuss the feedback once they've

17. Donovan, *10 Core Practices*, 119.
18. Donovan, *10 Core Practices*, 119.
19. Donovan, *10 Core Practices*, 119.

had a chance to read through it. Give them time to read and digest your comments in private before discussing any of it with you. The writer may not need to discuss the work with you at a later point, but it would be nice for them to know that you've left that door open in case they feel they could benefit from a conversation. True neighbor love says, I'll help you the way I would want to be helped, and often a follow-up conversation is exactly what we need.

CONCLUSION

Whether you are giving or receiving feedback, the goal is the same—to improve the work. As receivers we would do well to assume the best of our reviewers, and as reviewers we would do well to love our writing neighbors by providing critiques that help more than they hurt. Sometimes we may have a work returned to us with no feedback, just a rejection letter. But when feedback is provided, it is to be appreciated as a gift. Even harsh feedback can turn out to be helpful and deserves to be considered. Neither rejection letters nor harsh feedback should keep us from writing. As we said from the outset of this book, we academics write because we believe we have something to say that positively contributes to the scholarly conversation. You have something to say, and your colleagues in your field would benefit from your work. Rejections are setbacks that can be overcome by addressing the issues highlighted by reviewers. Critical feedback is not something to be feared. It may be uncomfortable, and even painful, in the short term, but in the long run it will improve your work if you are open to it and not afraid of it.

THE NEXT LEVEL

1. What is the point of critical feedback?

_____

_____

_____

2. Look at the last critique you received (either from a reviewer, professor, or peer). Which phrases hurt your ego? Why did those phrases hurt your ego? Do you feel as though you should have known better than to make that mistake, or did those phrases attack the writer and not the written word? It may be helpful to alter your reviewer's wording. If the phrases attacked the writer (e.g., "You are unclear"), rewrite them to focus on the writing (e.g., "This sentence is unclear"). If they include evaluative language, rewrite them with descriptive language.

3. After reading through negative criticism, how long should you let that information sit before you begin to address it? How long is too long?

4. How does thinking about receiving and providing feedback in terms of neighbor love change your attitude about receiving feedback? About giving feedback?

10

Participate in Professional Conferences

Good writers are always seeking to grow in their craft, and one of the key venues for such growth is professional conferences. They offer opportunities not only to participate as spectators or as attendees but also, more importantly, to present academic papers in front of peers. For me (Ben), this means attending and participating in conferences like the Evangelical Theological Society, the Evangelical Missiological Society, the Institute for Biblical Research, and the Society of Biblical Literature. The ability to network and rub shoulders with people whom you respect and admire can be extremely beneficial: listening to them present papers; asking questions from their stimulating (or even not so stimulating) papers; and interacting with them in and out of sessions. Anne Huff agrees: "The most exciting academic conversations typically take place at professional meetings and other face-to-face encounters."[1]

So, yes, attend professional conferences. But even better, participate in professional conferences. That means, at least for me, reading an academic paper at a conference whenever possible. Knowing that

---

1. Anne Sigismund Huff, *Writing for Scholarly Publication* (Thousand Oaks, CA: Sage, 1999), 96.

I will stand before my peers and present a paper causes me to be more diligent, forcing me to improve my essay. With experts present, I can't wing it and offer a paper that is still rough around the edges. No, I work and work until I have a polished essay that is ready for publication.

WHY ATTEND A CONFERENCE?

I (Adrianne) was surprised to find no mention of the benefits of attending professional conferences in any of the writing books on my bookshelf. While several of these books encourage writers to participate in writing workshops or groups, they do not discuss how conferences contribute to writing. However, a quick Google search returned several web pages of the top five, six, seven, eight, or ten reasons why one should attend academic conferences. Most of these reasons can be summarized under the umbrellas of *learn*, *listen*, and *talk*.

Learning is a major reason to attend a conference. Whether you attend as an observer or a presenter, there is so much to learn. As you hear papers being presented and attend the keynote addresses, you are exposing yourself to the latest trends and developments in your field. You hear new ideas and theories that may affect your current (or future) research. Conferences are like intensive classes that touch on a variety of topics. You may be surprised at what you learn. I (Adrianne) remember attending a literature conference early in my career. I was presenting a paper on a piece of seventeenth-century literature, and I intended to learn all I could from the other presenters on my panel and similar panels. However, as I glanced through the program, a paper on teaching composition caught my eye. I attended that presentation and learned ways to improve my composition classes—unexpected nuggets of wisdom as a bonus from attending a conference.

As you attend presentations and social events at conferences, you have multiple opportunities to meet like-minded individuals. Engaging in discussions with others is often encouraging and energizing. The people with whom you interact may become future collaborators on research and writing projects. Collaborations are great ways to build your reputation and increase the caliber of your work. At conferences you network and build professional relationships. Learning to network is an invaluable benefit of attending conferences.

Conferences also help you hone your listening skills. This happens naturally through networking conversations, and more formally when you present your research. The people who attend your talk are often interested and knowledgeable about your topic. During your paper's question-and-answer session, they may provide helpful feedback and ask questions that you had not considered but that may open doors for future research. Listen well to the questions and comments you receive. Take notes. Be sure to get the audience member's name so that you can follow up if needed (which is also an avenue for networking).

I (Ben) vividly recall giving a paper on 1 John 5:21 ("Little children, keep yourselves from idols") at the Evangelical Theological Society several years ago. After the paper and the question-and-answer session, a small, elderly gentleman walked up to me from the back of the room. As he approached, I noticed that this person was I. Howard Marshall, a New Testament scholar from the University of Aberdeen. Not only was he a world-class scholar, but he also had written a commentary on the Johannine Epistles. Anticipating that he might offer me feedback or critique, I grabbed a pen and was ready. He then gave me three helpful critiques that I wrote down and later incorporated before I submitted the essay to a journal, which published it. Don't underestimate the value of attending and reading papers at professional conferences. As you attend talks, listen to the questions and comments so that you become more familiar with the current academic conversation and can contribute to it in person and in your writing.

Learning and listening are great reasons to attend conferences, and you can do both without presenting, but we think your opportunities for learning and listening increase if you present your own work. The most compelling reason for a writer to participate in academic conferences is to talk. Present your own work to your peers. Overcome your fears of presenting or of sharing your work by reading your paper. Doing so helps you develop your communication skills, which in turn will help your writing. It also helps you build your confidence as an academic. Presentations may also lead to opportunities for publication. Conferences often publish their proceedings. Some of these are refereed publications, and some are not. Either way, presenting and publishing through conferences will strengthen your curriculum vitae and make a worthwhile investment in your future.

So find a conference that fits with your research interests and make plans to attend. Better yet, make plans to present your work. If a national conference seems too overwhelming, seek out a regional conference. You do not have to wait until graduation to participate in conferences. Attend as a student. Present as a student. If you feel intimidated or unsure, ask to tag along with your academic adviser to the next conference she is attending. Good academic advisers are already encouraging you to present your work at conferences. Heed your adviser's good advice. Learn, listen, and talk!

PREPARING TO PRESENT

If you present your work at a conference (and we really think you should), you'll find additional benefits as you work through the process of preparation and presentation. Some of the most helpful, but often less considered, benefits are brevity and timeliness. Submitting an abstract for consideration forces you to create an elevator pitch for your current work. What is your focus and why is that important in 250 to 500 words? The abstract-writing process helps you zero in on a thesis statement that can be covered in the twenty-to-thirty-minute presentation window, and it helps you narrow the focus of your research into something that you can easily discuss with others. I (Adrianne) often find that significant aspects of my abstracts become key sentences in the introduction and conclusion of my presentations and the articles that follow. Of course, as with any writing project—even a short abstract—you will produce a better product if you go through the writing, feedback, and rewriting process we have discussed in previous chapters.

In addition to enabling you to share the elevator pitch of your work in networking situations, presenting your work forces you to produce by a deadline. There's no extension given on conference presentations. You present what you have, knowing you are building your reputation and your curriculum vitae. There are usually several months between submission acceptance and the conference date, and an acceptance spurs you on to use your time wisely during those months. You get the necessary chunk of research done and you write, solicit feedback, and rewrite.

As you prepare to present your work, you should always read your paper out loud in private *before* you read your paper in public. In fact, it is beneficial to read out loud *any* paper you write. As Gary Provost notes, "Before you turn in anything you have written—whether to a teacher or an editor—read aloud every word."[2] When you orally practice presenting your paper, something happens that helps you recognize weaknesses that otherwise might have been missed. Certain phrases sound odd, omitted words become evident, redundancies are heard, and gaps in the general flow are felt. Patricia Goodson explains: "[Reading our work aloud] intensifies our own experience of our own words through multiple channels of perception. We don't just see them with our eyes and understand them with our minds; we feel them with our mouths and hear them in our ears—and indeed experience them proprioceptively in our bodies."[3]

You may end up changing words or phrases so that your presentation reads more like a talk than an academic paper. Short sentences, defined jargon terms, and an easy-to-follow pace will contribute to audience understanding. As you practice reading aloud, time your talk. If you are over the allotted time set by the conference, cut your work to fit the time. Don't simply read faster. You want your audience

2. Gary Provost, *100 Ways to Improve Your Writing: Proven Professional Techniques for Writing with Style and Power* (New York: Berkley, 2019), 153.

3. Patricia Goodson, *Becoming an Academic Writer: 50 Exercises for Paced, Productive, and Powerful Writing*, 2nd ed. (Thousand Oaks, CA: Sage, 2017), 136, citing Peter Elbow, *Vernacular Eloquence: What Speech Can Bring to Writing* (New York: Oxford University Press, 2012), 237. Natalie Goldberg agrees, "It is important to read aloud what you write." *Wild Mind: Living the Writer's Life* (New York: Bantam, 1990), 81. Andrew T. Le Peau similarly comments, "Many writers are wise to read their work aloud to themselves as part of the rewriting process. That way we engage our hearing, which can reveal grammatical errors, repetition of words, awkward phrasing, or unintentional rhyme. It also forces us to slow down so we can notice problems more easily." *Write Better: A Lifelong Editor on Craft, Art, and Spirituality* (Downers Grove, IL: InterVarsity, 2019), 85.

to understand your research and interact with your work. You don't want them to tune you out because they cannot follow your pace. We encourage you to read your paper to a few colleagues before you attend your conference. They will be able to give you helpful feedback concerning your presentation style and content.

We have talked much throughout this book about the importance of feedback. That is because constructive feedback is one of the most helpful tools for any writer. As noted above, presenting your work at a conference provides you with immediate feedback. You don't have to wait for an emailed written review; you receive questions and comments that you can interact with in the moment. Be sure to have a pen or pencil with you so that you can write everything down, even the comments or questions that you think are somewhat off-point. Write them down anyway. They may lead to future research or end up becoming great answers to various "So what?" questions. The feedback you receive during your presentation's question-and-answer portion can also lead to further discussions after the panel, during a conference social event, or over a meal. These types of conversation not only provide helpful information for your work; they also become key networking events and often open the doors for future collaborations. Feedback and further discussion are invaluable benefits from presenting.

Another invaluable benefit is that presenting at a conference improves your confidence in thinking and writing. You know your research, and you know the scholarly conversation surrounding your topic. At a conference, you discuss what you know—out loud and in front of people. When they ask you questions, you answer them, or you admit that you are intrigued by a perspective you had not considered. The experience of presenting and talking about your work teaches you that you know quite a bit about your topic. It teaches you that you can get off the bench and get in the game—and actually play. You see yourself contributing to the larger scholarly conversation, and this boosts your confidence as an academic.

If you have the opportunity to contribute to the proceedings of the conference, you will submit your paper, receive feedback, revise, and resubmit. This too boosts your confidence as an academic and encourages you to present again. With the confidence boost, you are also more likely to submit an article for publication in a refereed journal. Academic work tends to beget academic work; and when your conference presentations lead to article write-ups, you get yourself into a great cycle. Additionally, the connections you make at conferences may open doors for you to participate in special issues of academic journals that focus on your research area. Such issues are often filled by invitation only. If the editor does not know you or your work, she cannot be expected to invite you to participate in a special issue. Conferences are ideal places to make your work (and yourself) known. You not only open the door to invitations to participate in special issues, but you may also be invited to speak at other events, participate in panel discussions, or review article submissions for various journals because of your expertise. All these opportunities improve your confidence as an academic and build your curriculum vitae. In other words, they are exercises in becoming a strong academic.

CONCLUSION

As a student or professional in academia, it is vital that you attend and participate in academic conferences. We hope this chapter has persuaded you to get involved in a conference or two. Participating is a great way to grow as a researcher and presenter. You will come back to your normal routine refreshed and inspired with new ideas to add to your classroom lectures or assignments. But most importantly, conference participation makes you a better communicator, which makes you a better writer. Opportunities to contribute your work in written form to published conference proceedings are chances to hone your craft. And let's face it, it can be a lot of fun to talk for hours with other people who have interests similar to your own. That's great networking! No one is bored. Instead, everyone is energized. So get involved in academic conferences and grow as a presenter, a writer, and an academic scholar.

THE NEXT LEVEL

1. Do some research online and talk to your adviser or mentor to find a few conferences in the upcoming year that dovetail with your research interests.

   a. What are these conferences?

   b. When and where are these conferences being held?

   c. When are the deadlines to submit abstracts?

Name of Conference	Date of Conference	Location	Abstract Deadline

2. Choose one of the options above and commit to submitting an abstract and attending the conference. Attend even if your abstract is not accepted, so that you can become familiar with conference work and begin to network with like-minded scholars. In the table above, circle the conference you will attend. Put the abstract deadline and conference dates in your calendar. Tell your adviser or colleague of your plans so they can exert positive peer pressure and provide helpful feedback as the deadlines approach.

3. If you chose not to attend a conference this year (and we think this is a mistake), why are you not attending? What steps can you take this year that will enable you to attend next year? Keep in mind that many schools and conferences offer financial support for students and faculty for participating in professional activities. If you do not know what your school offers, do some research to find out. You might ask your adviser, your dean, or your provost.

11

Work to Improve Your Writing

Everyone can improve as a writer. We need to continually hone our skills to better communicate the truths and values we affirm. How do we do this? We must read and write—a lot. These are the best strategies to improve your writing, and your writing can always be improved. Good writers never stop reading and writing no matter how many publications they have under their belts. In any mode of communication, good models and continued practice lead to improvement.

READ GOOD WRITERS

In chapter 2 we encouraged you to always keep reading materials with you. We hope you are doing that and that you are reading good authors. Those good authors need not be limited to your field of research, although you should be reading good authors in your field. Read classics. Read modern books. Read those who have been able to write effectively or passionately or winsomely.[1] William Zinsser admits, "If anyone asked me how I learned to write, I'd say I learned

---

1. See Mortimer J. Adler and Charles Van Doren, *How to Read a Book: The Classic Guide to Intelligent Reading* (New York: Touchstone, 1972); and Karen Swallow

by reading the men and women who were doing the kind of writing I wanted to do and trying to figure out how they did it."[2] Stephen King similarly advises, "If you want to be a writer, you must do two things above all others: read a lot and write a lot. There's no way around these two things that I'm aware of, no shortcut. . . . If you don't have time to read, you don't have time (or the tools) to write. Simple as that."[3]

For King, "read a lot" is the "Great Commandment" for writers.[4] Why? Because reading

> creates an ease and intimacy with the process of writing. . . . Constant reading will pull you into a place (a mind-set, if you like the phrase) where you can write eagerly and without self-consciousness. It also offers you a constantly growing knowledge of what has been done and what hasn't; what is trite and what is fresh, what works and what just lies there dying (or dead) on the page. The more you read, the less apt you are to make a fool of yourself with your pen or word processor.[5]

If you want to know how to write a scholarly essay, read scholarly essays. But don't read for content alone; pay attention to what made that essay so effective.[6] Reading critically will help you not only to

---

Prior, *On Reading Well: Finding the Good Life through Great Books* (Grand Rapids: Brazos, 2018).

2. William Zinsser, *On Writing Well: The Classic Guide to Writing Nonfiction*, 7th ed., rev. and updated (New York: Harper Perennial, 2006), 34. Patricia Goodson likewise comments, "Reading other authors' good writing is an important ingredient in the recipe for writing well." *Becoming an Academic Writer: 50 Exercises for Paced, Productive, and Powerful Writing*, 2nd ed. (Thousand Oaks, CA: Sage, 2017), 41. Nijay K. Gupta echoes this same sentiment: "We all know the best writers are avid readers." *The Writer: A Guide to Research, Writing, and Publishing in Biblical Studies* (Eugene, OR: Cascade Books, 2022), 4.

3. Stephen King, *On Writing: A Memoir of the Craft* (New York: Scribner, 2000), 145, 147.

4. King, *On Writing*, 151.

5. King, *On Writing*, 150.

6. Emphasizing the importance of reading, Mike Wallace and Alison Wray state, "Reading is the first step toward writing. Scholarly writing would hardly count as scholarly if it ignored what other scholars had written on the topic. Scholarly writing usually includes an account that synthesizes and challenges previous research and puts forward new ideas." "Scholarly Reading as a Model for Scholarly Writing," in

recognize the strategies of good writing but also to become more profitably critical of your own writing.

READ BOOKS ON WRITING

As you begin to pay attention to the elements that make an essay or book in your field effective, you will start to notice that such works are easy to follow or understand. They flow smoothly from one point to the next and are organized in a way that is easy for the reader to digest. You are noticing elements of style, clarity, and grace, but you do not have to scavenge for these elements of good writing. You can access books on writing to improve your own work. Even professional writers use such books to hone their work. Melissa Donovan admits that books about writing have given her "tons of tips and techniques about the writing process that [she] otherwise never would have discovered."[7]

We listed several helpful books on writing in chapter 2 and now add the following to that list:

Harris, Robert. *Writing with Clarity and Style: A Guide to Rhetorical Devices for Contemporary Writers.* **2nd edition. New York: Routledge, 2017.** Harris works to help his readers communicate their ideas in clear ways that are not boring. He covers a multitude of writing venues, from emails to blogs to books, and examines both the sentence-level details and the big picture of communication.

Provost, Gary. *100 Ways to Improve Your Writing: Proven Professional Techniques for Writing with Style and Power.* **Updated edition. New York: Berkley, 2019.** Provost includes several sections on punctuation and style but begins with helpful information about improving your writing process and overcoming writer's block.

The Handbook of Scholarly Writing and Publishing, ed. Tonette S. Rocco and Tim Hatcher (San Francisco: Jossey-Bass, 2011), 44.

7. Melissa Donovan, *10 Core Practices for Better Writing* (San Francisco: Swan Hatch, 2013), 16.

Williams, Joseph M., and Joseph Bizup. *Style: The Basics of Clarity and Grace*. 5th edition. London: Pearson, 2014. This book is one of the writing classics. It is short, accessible to all levels of writers, and pointedly helpful. In fact, the inside cover includes "Ten Principles for Writing Clearly," which serves as a quick resource for improving your writing.

Williams, Joseph M., and Joseph Bizup. *Style: Lessons in Clarity and Grace*. 13th edition. London: Pearson, 2020. While similar to the other style books, this text is longer, going into a bit more detail than the others mentioned.

These texts can become your writing teachers that you can revisit time after time, paper after paper, as you continue in your writing career. Many of the rules for good writing presented in these books express principles that we may unconsciously know but may have been unable to articulate. We recognize that a work implementing these principles is enjoyable or easy to read, but we may not be able to explain why. Books on the craft of writing articulate them for us and help us to consciously include them in our own writing.

WRITE: PRACTICE WHAT YOU LEARN

While many stylebooks say the same thing in different ways, it is helpful to read several because hearing the lesson in different ways helps it take hold in our minds. Below is some of the practical advice that many writing books discuss and that you may have heard before. Because we see our students struggle with these, we want to highlight them here:

- *Know your audience.* A well-known saying among publishers is, "A book that is for everyone is for no one."[8] Awareness of your audience determines your vocabulary, writing style, organizational structure, length, title, and use of notes (no notes, footnotes, or endnotes).

8. See, e.g., Andrew T. Le Peau, *Write Better: A Lifelong Editor on Craft, Art, and Spirituality* (Downers Grove, IL: InterVarsity, 2019), 25.

- *Have a clear thesis statement.* Michael Kibbe writes, "Your thesis is the heart and soul of your paper." Therefore, he says, "Every single word, phrase and paragraph in your paper should contribute to your thesis. If something in your paper doesn't contribute to your thesis, cut it out."[9]
- *Avoid the passive voice.* Write active sentences so that the reader can know who is accomplishing the action (avoid "it was" or "there were"). Zinsser likewise writes, "Use active verbs unless there is no comfortable way to get around using the passive."[10] Also, watch the tenses: don't shift tenses unless it is necessary or purposeful.
- *Use strong active verbs.* For example, "There were a great number of dead leaves lying on the ground" becomes "Dead leaves covered the ground."[11] This often involves changing a "to be" verb into a verb of action or motion. Provost offers the following example: "A grandfather clock *was* in one corner, and three books *were* on top of it." He then provides the following sample containing active verbs: "A grandfather clock *towered* in one corner, and three books *lay* on top of it."[12]
- *Avoid the overuse of adverbs, adjectives, nominalizations, and prepositional phrases.* Instead of employing adverbs to add emphasis to verbs, find stronger verbs to convey your intent. Instead of describing someone who "ravenously ate" his food, use "devoured." Provost writes, "Most adverbs are just adjectives with -ly tacked on the end, and the majority of them should be shoveled into a truck and hauled off to the junk yard."[13]

9. Michael Kibbe, *From Topic to Thesis: A Guide to Theological Research* (Downers Grove, IL: InterVarsity, 2016), 87. See also Wayne Booth et al., *The Craft of Research*, 4th ed. (Chicago: University of Chicago Press, 2016).

10. Zinsser, *On Writing Well*, 67. George Orwell quipped, "Never use the passive voice where you can use the active." Orwell, quoted in Roy Peter Clark, *Writing Tools: 55 Essential Strategies for Every Writer* (New York: Little, Brown, 2016), 20. See also Helen Sword, *Stylish Academic Writing* (Cambridge, MA: Harvard University Press, 2012), 27.

11. William Strunk Jr. and E. B. White, *The Elements of Style*, 4th ed. (Boston: Pearson, 2000), 19.

12. Gary Provost, *100 Ways to Improve Your Writing: Proven Professional Techniques for Writing with Style and Power* (New York: Berkley, 2019), 73.

13. Provost, *100 Ways to Improve Your Writing*, 75. "Most adverbs are unnecessary" (Zinsser, *On Writing Well*, 68). "The adverb is not your friend" (King, *On Writing*,

112 Christian Academic Writing

Often adverbs restate the meaning inherent in the verb. For
example, consider: "blared loudly," "clench tightly," or "totally
flabbergasted." Also, beware of using abstract adjectives and
nominalizations (that is, verbs that are turned into nouns; e.g.,
"The *judgment* of God is . . ." is better as "God judges . . ."").
Sword notes that too often "authors use prepositions to string
together long sequences of abstract nouns," which clutter the
sentence and obscure the meaning.[14]

- *Avoid slang.* Nancy Vyhmeister explains, "Idiomatic expressions are out of place. . . . Research language is standard, not
  colloquial; it never uses slang." She also reminds us, "The language of the pulpit is not the language of the thesis."[15]

- *Use a thesaurus for variation.* Roy Peter Clark proclaims, "All
  of us possess a reading vocabulary as big as a lake but draw
  from a writing vocabulary as small as a pond."[16]

- *Be simple.* Simplicity is king, but it is also difficult. This is true
  for sentences. A general rule I (Ben) follow is this: if a sentence
  takes more than two lines, it is too long. Divide it into two or
  more sentences. Paula LaRocque insists that "when a sentence
  grows to 20 words or so, the writer should start seeking a way
  to end it."[17]

- *Be clear.* Don't write in such a way that only you know what
  you've said (and then only barely). There is no virtue in sound-
  ing smart but failing to communicate. Andrew Le Peau states,
  "We often think that sophisticated vocabulary makes us seem
  more impressive and intelligent. It's a way, we think, of making ourselves seem credible, giving us an air of authority. The
  opposite is true."[18] Daniel Oppenheimer, a professor at Carn-

---

124). "A well-written research paper will not contain as many adverbs and adjectives
as nouns and verbs" (Nancy Jean Vyhmeister, *Your Guide to Writing Quality Research
Papers: For Students of Religion and Theology* [Grand Rapids: Zondervan, 2014], 169).

14. Sword, *Stylish Academic Writing*, 55.

15. Vyhmeister, *Your Guide to Writing Quality Research Papers*, 169, 170.

16. Clark, *Writing Tools*, 70.

17. Paula LaRocque, *The Book on Writing: The Ultimate Guide to Writing Well*
(Arlington, TX: Grey & Guvnor, 2003), 5.

18. Le Peau, *Write Better*, 48. Erwin H. Epstein writes, "New scholars commonly
make the mistake of thinking that the more words used to express a thought, the

egie Mellon, offers the following example: "Consequences of Erudite Vernacular Utilized Irrespective of Necessity: Problems with Using Long Words Needlessly."[19]

In sum, as Zinsser states, "The secret of good writing is to strip every sentence down to its cleanest components. Every word that serves no function, every long word that could be a short word, every adverb that carries the same meaning that's already in the verb, every passive construction that leaves the reader unsure of who is doing what—these are the thousand and one adulterants that weaken the strength of a sentence."[20] A good writer should always be seeking to become a better writer.

READ BOOKS ON WRITING IN YOUR DISCIPLINE

In addition to books that will help you improve the mechanics of your craft, read books on the writing craft that pertain to your general field of work and research to gain insight on how you can write while earning a living in the academic world or in ministry. We realize that it is not likely that you will find a book on writing about the Trinity in theological studies or writing about heaven in academic journals. Writing craft books are not that specific, but you can find resources that will help you better understand how to write academic articles or how to write for ministry. As we mentioned earlier, most academic writers are not professional writers. Instead, they are professionals who write. Similarly, ministers who write for more general audiences are professionals who write. It does not take much research to find books on writing in your discipline.

more cogent that thought will be. . . . [They] err on the side of wordiness, thinking that more words will yield greater semblance of legitimacy to their work. In fact, excessive verbiage dampens the meaning the author wishes to convey." "Writing with Authority: Pitfalls and Pit Stops," in *The Handbook of Scholarly Writing and Publishing*, ed. Tonette S. Rocco and Tim Hatcher (San Francisco: Jossey-Bass, 2011), 92.

19. Daniel Oppenheimer, quoted in Le Peau, *Write Better*, 49. Here is another example of how not to write: "Objective consideration of contemporary phenomena compels the conclusion that success or failure in competitive activities exhibits no tendency to be commensurate with innate capacity, but that a considerable element of the unpredictable must invariably be taken into account." LaRocque, *Book on Writing*, 15.

20. Zinsser, *On Writing Well*, 6–7.

If you are an academic, two types of resources will aid you as you write for the academy: those on the mechanics of writing and those on strategies for writing. Books like *An Insider's Guide to Academic Writing: A Brief Rhetoric* encourage readers to develop academic arguments.[21] That book goes on to break down writing in the humanities, social sciences, natural sciences, and other fields. Why? Because academic writing in the humanities is different from academic writing in the natural sciences. Different academic communities have different disciplinary conventions. For example, opinions and hedging of opinions are accepted and even encouraged in the humanities, whereas the natural sciences demand more objectivity, even to the point of allowing sentences in the passive voice.

In addition to resources on how to write, others focus on writing for specific types of publications. For example, *Writing for Academic Journals*, by Rowena Murray, helps readers figure out what kinds of journals to target and walks them through developing an argument, outlining, drafting, and revising.[22] For those who are interested in writing a monograph, Mauricio Fau's *How to Write a Monograph* may prove helpful.[23] He not only walks writers through the process, but he also explains the differences between monographs and other long works, such as dissertations. Nijay Gupta's *The Writer: A Guide to Research, Writing, and Publishing in Biblical Studies* provides a step-by-step guide, especially written for those in biblical studies.[24] In addition to resources such as Murray's, Fau's, and Gupta's, academic writers should be reading (and rereading) publication guidelines for the journals or publishing houses that interest them. Publishers won't take your work seriously if you do not take their guidelines seriously.

Besides honing your craft by reading resources about writing in your general discipline and about writing journal pieces or monographs (or blogs or popular magazine articles, for that matter), it is

---

21. Susan Miller-Cochran, Roy Stamper, and Stacey Cochran, *An Insider's Guide to Academic Writing: A Brief Rhetoric*, 3rd ed. (Boston: Bedford/St. Martin's, 2022).

22. Rowena Murray, *Writing for Academic Journals*, 4th ed. (London: Open University Press, 2020).

23. Mauricio Fau, *How to Write a Monograph* (self-published, 2021).

24. Nijay K. Gupta, *The Writer: A Guide to Research, Writing, and Publishing in Biblical Studies* (Eugene, OR: Cascade Books, 2022).

also helpful to read works that encourage writers who have a day job. Books like Robert Boice's *Professors as Writers* can foster productivity with strategies to help you block out time to write.[25] (Such information is also found in Murray's book.) Eviatar Zerubavel's *The Clockwork Muse* also provides useful advice for moving from idea to finished work.[26] For ministers or teachers, *Writing for Life and Ministry* is a practical guide to help you understand your readers and move forward in the writing process.[27]

CONCLUSION

As we said at the outset of this chapter, it takes two practices to improve your writing: reading and writing. And these practices take time, so use your time wisely. Keep reading materials with you so that you can read about writing while waiting for the dentist or sitting in carpool, or during any other "downtime" you have in your week. But don't stop with reading about writing. You must write and keep writing. The more you apply the information you have read to your writing, the better your work will become, and the more confident you will become as a writer. Practice breeds productivity, and productivity breeds improvement, and improvement breeds confidence, which will, in turn, feed your desire to write more. Put yourself on this positive writing spiral by reading and writing.

THE NEXT LEVEL

1. What book are you reading right now that is outside your specific field of research?

---

25. Robert Boice, *Professors as Writers: A Self-Help Guide to Productive Writing*, 4th ed. (Stillwater, OK: New Forums Press, 1990).

26. Eviatar Zerubavel, *The Clockwork Muse: A Practical Guide to Writing Theses, Dissertations, and Books* (Cambridge, MA: Harvard University Press, 1999).

27. Brandon J. O'Brien, *Writing for Life and Ministry: A Practical Guide to the Writing Process for Teachers and Preachers* (Chicago: Moody, 2020).

If you are not currently reading a book outside your field, what classic or modern work would you like to read?

_____

Put this book by your bed, in your bathroom, or in your car—whichever place affords you the most downtime in your week. If you eat lunch alone, read this as you eat.

2. Choose a book on writing style to read. Which will you start with?

_____

Put it on your desk and read one chapter or section each day at the beginning of your writing time. Do not spend more than ten minutes reading. Let the topic of the one section you read each day spill into your writing that day.

3. Choose a book on writing in your discipline or in your profession. Which did you choose?

_____

Put it in your bathroom and read one short section each morning as you brush your teeth. We hope this will encourage you at the beginning of each day to hone your writing for your discipline and redeem time for writing.

12

Finish What You Start

I (Ben) once heard about a professor who had perhaps dozens of essays or chapters stored in his filing cabinet that he was patiently waiting to finish and publish when the time was right. The rationale behind this delayed approach is that you don't want to rush your work but want to let it simmer and mature—wait until you have mastered your topic and then, and only then, release it to the world for consideration. Although there may be some value to such thinking, we are not persuaded that it is the best approach. On the contrary, we urge budding authors (as well as seasoned authors) to finish the work they have started—and by "finish," we mean "publish."

In an important communicative way, a work is not finished until it finds its way into a journal or book. Why labor so hard to research your topic and write your essay if, at the end of the day, it is merely stuffed into the recesses of your filing cabinet? Didn't you have something important to say? Weren't you attempting to correct a misunderstanding of a significant truth? Didn't you offer a fresh perspective that would open new avenues of dialogue and discussion? As far as I (Ben) can recall, I have never written an academic essay, chapter, or monograph that was not published. Once I finish writing an essay, I'm only halfway done. I proof and edit the work until it is ready to be sent to a journal (or publisher).

WHY PUBLISH?

Publications are good for both the writer and the larger academic discipline. Rowena Murray offers the following ten reasons a scholar should publish in an academic journal:[1]

1. Career progression
2. Gaining recognition for the work you have done
3. Stopping someone else from taking credit for your work or using your materials
4. Personal satisfaction of completing a new goal
5. Setting yourself a new challenge
6. Helping your students to gain recognition for their work
7. Learning how to write to a high standard
8. Contributing to knowledge
9. Building your institution's status
10. Developing a profile

While we do not disagree with any of her reasons, we would categorize public, professional, and personal reasons separately and prioritize a few over others.

As mentioned above, writing is about communication. Sometimes writing helps an individual organize and clarify his or her own thoughts, and we recognize the self-communicative value of writing. However, we believe that research should be shared with others. This public reason for publishing is founded on the belief that when we share research and discoveries, a body of knowledge grows, a discipline grows and advances. Not publishing your research hides it from the rest of the world when others could benefit from the work you have done. Thus, we urge academics to publish in order to contribute their work to their field of study. Sharing knowledge is important for all societies, academic and otherwise. As Helen Sword explains, "Writing for publication is, after all, a deeply human act: we write to communicate our research findings *to* other people."[2]

---

1. Rowena Murray, *Writing for Academic Journals*, 4th ed. (London: Open University Press, 2020), 6.
2. Helen Sword, *Air & Light & Time & Space: How Successful Academics Write* (Cambridge, MA: Harvard University Press, 2017), 106.

Most of the other reasons to publish your research fall into the professional and personal categories, but those are no less important. Professionally, a writer publishes to build her reputation. For better or worse, most academics are judged, at least in part, by their publications or lack thereof. Publishing demonstrates your professional commitment to your work and can help an academic achieve recognition and promotion. As you build your reputation, you will have opportunities to work with other colleagues and students. Publishing is an ideal way to help your coauthors build their reputations as well. Reputation is an important part of the academic world. This includes your reputation, that of your colleagues and students, and that of your department and institution. When you publish, your department and the larger institution are recognized as venues for current research, and this can help a program or school grow. In other words, publishing is good for your career and for the people and institution you work with and for.

On a more personal level, publishing makes you a better researcher and writer. You improve your skills by participating in the activity. Through critiques, you grow and improve. By doing, you learn and you encourage yourself to keep researching and writing. There's nothing like seeing your work in print to make you want to continue to research and publish. You build your confidence as a researcher and writer through publishing, and you position yourself to be a mentor to others. As academics, we do not want to hide any of our skills; we want to share them with others to improve our academic disciplines.

STRATEGIES FOR FINISHING

Despite these public, professional, and personal reasons for academics to publish their work, often the step from completed draft to submission is the hardest step. Not long ago someone posted this on Twitter: "Found an essay I wrote in 2017 that's needed either a makeover for publication or a trip to the dust bin, so I finally caved. I've said it before and I'll say it again, getting an article from 'basically written' to 'submittable' is one of the hardest hurdles." For some reason, many people cannot make it past this step. Why? Insecurity? Fear of failure? Fear of style guides and footnotes? Busyness? There are valid excuses, but most excuses are simply attempts to justify our hesitancy (or failure) to push through the final step of the writing process.

It is important to finish—completely finish—what we have started. However, the temptation to give up (or give in) is not unique to the field of writing. Look around your home, your neighborhood, and the larger community. How many unfinished projects can you find? You may have a knitting project, a painting, or a wood carving that you never finished. You may have a neighbor who wants to restore the antique car in his or her garage but never has gotten around to it. You may see walls half built or land, once cleared for building, with saplings now growing on it. People have a hard time bringing projects to fruition.

A quick internet search on "how to finish what you start" returns over eleven thousand results, which indicates that this problem is common to many. Several of these web pages encourage people to confront their own self-criticism and look at the situation honestly. Many hindrances to finishing were discussed in chapter 4 when we worked to dispel writing myths.

One common roadblock to publishing is procrastination. We have the article ready but keep putting off researching an appropriate journal. This type of stalling can be especially strong if you have been rejected by the first journal to which you submitted your manuscript. We urge you to always have a backup plan. While you absolutely should submit to your preferred journal first, we think you should also know your next step in case the answer is no. When I (Adrianne) decided to submit an article to the premier journal in my field, I knew it was a long shot. I also knew that if that national journal did not accept my article, I would revise according to whatever feedback I received and submit it to one of its regional affiliates. This plan kept me from wallowing too long in my rejected state because I had a plan for moving on.

Another reason we abandon a writing project just before the finish line (publication) could be that the excitement of a "new" project has worn off. The project no longer feels new. It's done, or mostly done, and reformatting it to a specific style guide is no fun. You might find yourself organizing your desk or dusting your bookshelves to avoid that drudgery. Or you may find that the publisher does not accept submissions over a certain number of words, and your article is over the limit. Which two hundred (or two thousand!) words should you cut out? This kind of work is tedious and difficult and easy to put on the back burner. Susan Perry, who has studied writing flow, points out that "tedium and drudgery" often stop writers from continuing.[3] Eviatar Zerubavel suggests that this problem often comes up when we work too long on a given project. He argues, "What may have once been a source of great pleasure and excitement can become a source of boredom and frustration."[4] Tackle the lack of excitement at the finish line by building fun back into your task. Reward yourself for each milestone, including formatting, with your favorite snack or a stroll around campus. Dangle a carrot out in front of yourself to help you cross that finish line.

For many of us a realistic timeline with mini-milestone dates set can be helpful. I (Adrianne) am a list maker and a calendar follower. While I use electronic and visual calendars, I find the poster-sized dry-erase calendar on my office wall to be the best encouragement to help me keep my writing on track with my timeline. I write the mini milestones on that wall calendar, which shows four months—a whole semester—at a glance, and then see those mini milestones every day. This daily visual reminder encourages me to stay on track and finish because I see those submission deadlines from the beginning of the project.

As you work to create your own deadlines for your writing project(s), keep in mind that deadlines must be realistic or you will learn to ignore them. You know yourself, your schedule, your workload. Use this information to set realistic, attainable timelines that help you move your work from research and drafting to publishing.

Another helpful tip for staying on track for publishing is to have a writing friend who is willing to serve as your accountability partner. This person could be a mentor or a peer, but it is ideal to partner with

3. Susan K. Perry, "Five Ways to Finish What You Start (and Why You Often Don't)," *Psychology Today*, February 25, 2014, https://www.psychologytoday.com/us/blog/creating-in-flow/201402/5-ways-finish-what-you-start-and-why-you-often-dont.

4. Eviatar Zerubavel, *The Clockwork Muse: A Practical Guide to Writing Theses, Dissertations, and Books* (Cambridge, MA: Harvard University Press, 1999), 87.

someone who is also writing so that each of you can hold the other accountable. Accountability could include formal meetings each week or month in which you give updates on your progress and discuss your work, or it could be more organic in that you know one another's timelines and periodically check in with one another to ask if those deadlines are being met. Your writing accountability partner can even help you set a realistic and achievable timeline as they get to know you better and understand your work habits. Sometimes just knowing that someone else is going through the process that you are going through, with all the highs and lows, can be extremely helpful and encouraging, especially when you are writing behind closed doors.

OVERCOMING REJECTION

Perhaps the strongest roadblock to publishing is rejection. You work so hard on a manuscript and with high hopes send it to a publisher for review only to have it rejected. Rejection letters often come months after submission, so that not only are you discouraged by the rejection, but you may have also lost the excitement you once had over that manuscript. When rejection comes—and it comes to all—we say, "Press on!" In chapter 9, we briefly touched on the setbacks that rejections can bring but encouraged you that such setbacks can be overcome. We noted that the feedback offered by reviewers who reject your work can and should be addressed to improve the work.

Often the feedback is more about the writing than the methodology.[5] Do not feel like you have to throw out your work and start over. Instead, take the comments at face value and revise to improve your manuscript so that you can resubmit it. If a reviewer says that a paragraph or section of your paper adds nothing new to the scholarly conversation, you must reread your manuscript, paying close attention to that section. Is the reviewer correct so that you should cut that part, or is it important for your argument? If you believe you need that section, then acknowledge the reviewer's comments by saying something like, "This is a well-known, and possibly overused argument, but it bears on the present discussion because . . ." Explain

5. Murray, *Writing for Academic Journals*, 186.

your reasons for keeping it in and move on to the next comment for revision. Sometimes, reviewers ask for information that is beyond the scope of your paper. Honestly state that in your revision and move on. If you find it difficult to sift through reviewers' comments, go over them with your adviser, mentor, or writing accountability partner so you have help moving forward with your project. We offer these examples to encourage you that rejection can, and often should, lead to better writing. Writers become more thoughtful and more mindful because of their interactions with reviewers—members of their target audience. Better writing produces a better manuscript that should be resubmitted for publication.

CONCLUSION

Publication is the goal because, as we state at the outset of this chapter, you have something important to say. What you have to say needs to be heard in your discipline so that the discipline may advance. The best way to be heard is to publish. Publication should be part of your timeline from the outset of your project.

At the same time, we recognize it can be a struggle to go from the red zone into the end zone, to use a football analogy. But the points (public, personal, and professional) are worth the touchdown. As I (Adrianne) write this paragraph I feel tired. I've already written so much. Why did Ben and I decide on twelve chapters and not eleven? I want to be finished, but there's more work to do. The submission deadline is coming. Revisions will come after that, and months from now, maybe a year from now, we will have a published book. Right now, the red zone seems more like fifty yards than twenty, but the truth is we have more yards behind us than ahead. We believe we have something worth saying that will help other academics. (And I know that the reward waiting for me at the end of my writing session today is an order of hot, crispy, salty french fries!) When you get to the "end" and feel your energy dwindling, remind yourself of what lies behind you. You've done most of the hard work already, but your project does not end with the last word you type. You are not finished when the essay or book is finished. You must take the time to try to get it published. We want to hear what you have to say!

THE NEXT LEVEL

1. Why should you publish? List at least one strong professional reason and at least one strong personal reason.

   a. Professional reason(s)

   _____

   _____

   b. Personal reason(s)

   _____

   _____

2. What is the biggest roadblock that hinders you from pushing through to publication?

   _____

   _____

   _____

3. How will you work to overcome that roadblock?

   _____

   _____

   _____

4. Do you have something worth saying? The answer is *yes*!

   _____

   _____

   _____

Academic Religious Publishers

Publishing a book is not easy, especially if it is your first book. Sometimes the biggest challenge is identifying the best publisher for your content. In this appendix, we provide relevant information regarding thirty-one publishers, including (1) an overview of the publisher's history as well as the type of material they publish, (2) their website, (3) an email address, (4) a physical address, and (5) where to find submission guidelines (of course, some of this information is subject to change). Below is a list of the thirty-one publishers in alphabetical order followed by a more detailed summary of the information mentioned above.

1. Abingdon Press
2. Baker Academic
3. B&H Academic
4. Baylor University Press
5. Brazos Press
6. Cambridge University Press
7. Cascade Books
8. Concordia Publishing House
9. Crossway Books
10. Eerdmans Publishing Company
11. Eisenbrauns

12. Fortress Press

13. Good Book Company

14. Hendrickson Academic

15. InterVarsity Press

16. Kregel Publications

17. Lexham Press

18. Mohr Siebeck

19. Moody Publishers

20. Oxford University Press

21. Paulist Press

22. Peter Lang

23. Pickwick Publications

24. Presbyterian & Reformed Publishing (P&R)

25. Reformation Heritage Books (RHB)

26. Smyth & Helwys Books

27. Thomas Nelson

28. Tyndale House Publishers

29. Westminster John Knox Press

30. Wipf and Stock Publishers

31. Zondervan Academic

ABINGDON PRESS

Overview: Abingdon Press is an imprint of The United Methodist Publishing House, which has been in operation since 1789, making it one of the oldest publishing houses in the US. It publishes inspirational, professional, academic, and practical literature. This publisher accepts unsolicited manuscripts in the fields of Christian living, leadership, academic subjects, and church program resources.
Website: https://www.abingdonpress.com
Email: orders@abingdonpress.com
Address: 2222 Rosa L. Parks Boulevard, Nashville, TN 37228
Submission Guidelines: https://www.abingdonpress.com/submissions

BAKER ACADEMIC

Overview: Baker Academic is a division of Baker Publishing Group and serves both the academy and the church. Baker started as a Reformed and evangelical publisher and now publishes across the broader academic community with books that reflect historic Christianity and its contemporary expressions. They publish primary and supplementary textbooks, reference works, and scholarly monographs focusing on biblical studies, theology, ethics, cultural studies,

and church history as well as textbooks on Christian education, mission, ministry, literature, communication, philosophy, and psychology.
Website: http://bakerpublishinggroup.com/bakeracademic
Email: info@christianmanuscriptsubmissions.com
Address: 6030 East Fulton Road, Ada, MI 49301
Submission Guidelines: http://bakerpublishinggroup.com/contact /submission-policy

B&H (ACADEMIC)

Overview: B&H Academic is an imprint of B&H Publishing Group (a division of LifeWay) and was created in 2005 to provide resources for undergraduate and graduate theological education, as well as for pastors and ministry leaders. Its goal is to publish works that are biblically faithful and academically challenging and that promote the academy and build up the church.
Website: https://bhacademic.bhpublishinggroup.com
Email: bhacademic@lifeway.com
Address: 1 Lifeway Plaza, Nashville, TN 37234
Submission Guidelines: https://bhacademic.bhpublishinggroup.com /faqs

BAYLOR UNIVERSITY PRESS

Overview: Established in 1897, Baylor University Press is the academic publishing division of Baylor University and publishes forty academic titles every year. Baylor publishes technical academic work and textbooks that undergo rigorous peer review. Publishable topics include scriptural, historical, and theological studies of Christianity, Judaism, and Islam. Additionally, the press publishes works that investigate the relationship between religion and politics, sociology, anthropology, literature, philosophy, history, and culture.
Website: www.baylorpress.com
Email: bup_acquisitions@baylor.edu
Address: One Bear Place #97363, Waco, TX 76798-7363
Submission Guidelines: https://www.baylorpress.com/resources/pro spective-authors/proposal-requirements

BRAZOS PRESS

Overview: Brazos Press is a division of Baker Publishing Group and publishes across denominations. Consequently, Brazos authors represent various racial backgrounds and spiritual traditions. Brazos books are intellectual yet accessible, written with both skill and passion.
Website: http://www.bakerpublishinggroup.com/brazospress
Email: info@christianmanuscriptsubmissions.com
Address: 6030 East Fulton Road, Ada, MI 49301
Submission Guidelines: http://www.bakerpublishinggroup.com /brazospress/submitting-a-proposal

CAMBRIDGE UNIVERSITY PRESS (CUP)

Overview: CUP publishes more than 1,600 books and 380 journals each year in the humanities and sciences. It publishes research monographs, academic references, textbooks, and other books for professionals.
Website: https://www.cambridge.org/us/academic
Email: information@cambridge.org
Address: University Printing House, Shaftesbury Road, Cambridge CB2 8BS
Submission Guidelines: https://www.cambridge.org/authorhub /resources/publishing-guides-academic-authors

CASCADE BOOKS

Overview: Cascade is an imprint of Wipf and Stock Publishers. It publishes religious works that are academically rigorous with broad appeal and readability. These works target both the academy and faith communities, offering books in theology, biblical studies, religious history, spirituality, ministry, and cultural criticism.
Website: https://wipfandstock.com/search-results-grid/?imprint=cas cade-books
Email: proposal@wipfandstock.com
Address: 199 West 8th Avenue, Suite 3, Eugene, OR 97401-2960
Submission Guidelines: https://wipfandstock.com/submitting-a-pro posal/

CONCORDIA PUBLISHING HOUSE

Overview: Concordia Publishing House is the publishing division of The Lutheran Church–Missouri Synod. Their goal is to strengthen member churches by publishing nonfiction such as commentaries, curricula, and books related to Christian living.
Website: www.cph.org
Email: laura.lane@cph.org
Address: 3558 South Jefferson Avenue, Saint Louis, MO 63118-3968
Submission Guidelines: https://about.cph.org/manuscript-submission .html

CROSSWAY BOOKS

Overview: Crossway is a not-for-profit Christian ministry that exists to proclaim the gospel through publishing gospel-centered and Bible-centered content. They publish the English Standard Version of the Bible (2001) and are also interested in academic and professional volumes. They accept unsolicited manuscripts.
Website: https://www.crossway.org/
Email: submissions@crossway.org
Address: 1300 Crescent Street, Wheaton, IL 60187
Submission Guidelines: https://www.crossway.org/submissions/

EERDMANS PUBLISHING COMPANY

Overview: Eerdmans was founded in 1911 and is an independent publishing house. They publish religious texts, including academic books and reference works in theology, biblical studies, and religious history, as well as works related to spirituality and literature.
Website: https://www.eerdmans.com
Email: submissions@eerdmans.com
Address: 4035 Park East Court SE, Grand Rapids, MI 49546
Submission Guidelines: https://www.eerdmans.com/Pages/Item/2068 /Submission-Guidelines.aspx

EISENBRAUNS

Overview: Established in 1975, Eisenbrauns is an imprint of Penn State University Press (since 2017). They focus on titles related to ancient Near East studies, biblical studies, biblical archaeology, Assyriology, and linguistics.
Website: https://www.eisenbrauns.org/
Email: m.metzler@eisenbrauns.org
Address: 820 N. University Drive Usb 1, Suite C, University Park, PA 16802-1003
Submission Guidelines: https://www.eisenbrauns.org/books/author _resources/manuscript_guidelines.html

FORTRESS PRESS

Overview: Fortress Press is an imprint of 1517 Media and publishes compelling theological, biblical, and ethical works for the church.
Website: https://www.fortresspress.com
Address: 411 Washington Avenue N., 3rd Floor, Minneapolis, MN 55401
Submission Guidelines: https://www.fortresspress.com/info/submis sions

GOOD BOOK COMPANY

Overview: The Good Book Company is an evangelical publishing house that produces Bible-focused resources to promote, encourage, and equip the church. It focuses on books related to evangelism, Bible study, training, and Christian living.
Website: https://www.thegoodbook.com
Email: submissions@thegoodbook.com
Address: 1805 Sardis Road North, Suite 102, Charlotte, NC 28270
Submission Guidelines: https://www.thegoodbook.com/authors

HENDRICKSON ACADEMIC

Overview: Hendrickson Academic is an imprint of Hendrickson Publishing Group. It publishes works for the worldwide religious academic community on the Hebrew Bible and Hebrew language, ancient Near Eastern studies and archaeology, New Testament and Greek language, biblical theology, Judaism, patristics, church history, historical theology, practical theology, and religion and culture.
Website: https://hendricksonpublishinggroup.com/hendrickson-academic
Email: orders@hendricksonrose.com
Address: 3 Centennial Drive, Suite 100, Peabody, MA 01960
Submission Guidelines: Contact csresponse@tyndale.com

INTERVARSITY PRESS (IVP)

Overview: IVP is an extension of the InterVarsity Christian Fellowship USA and focuses on thoughtful books about church, culture, and mission that are produced with high academic rigor. IVP Academic is the academic imprint of IVP and publishes titles and textbooks that are relevant to the academy and the church.
Website: https://www.ivpress.com
Email: Contact form available on the website
Address: PO Box 1400, Downers Grove, IL 60515
Submission Guidelines: https://www.ivpress.com/submissions

KREGEL PUBLICATIONS

Overview: Kregel Publications is an evangelical company that has been providing resources for the church since 1949. It has a backlist of over one thousand titles in the following categories: Christian education, ministry, contemporary issues, fiction, Christian living, and biblical studies. Kregel Academic is an imprint of Kregel Publications, and Portavoz is their imprint that serves the Spanish-speaking church with over five hundred titles in print.
Website: https://www.kregel.com
Email: info@writersedgeservice.com

Address: 2450 Oak Industrial Drive NE, Grand Rapids, MI 49505
Submission Guidelines: https://www.kregel.com/contact-us/submis
sions-policy

LEXHAM PRESS

Overview: Lexham Press is owned by the parent company Faithlife
(which also owns Logos). It publishes pastoral and scholarly work
in biblical studies, Greek and Hebrew language resources, theology
(biblical, historical, and systematic), and ministry resources from an
evangelical perspective. Lexham Academic is their academic imprint.
Website: https://lexhampress.com
Email: editor@lexhampress.com
Address: 1313 Commercial Street, Bellingham, WA 98225
Submission Guidelines: https://lexhampress.com/manuscript-sub
mission

MOHR SIEBECK

Overview: Mohr Siebeck is an independent, family-owned publisher
that was founded in 1801. Its purpose is to publish academic works
of enduring quality. They also publish dissertations.
Website: https://www.mohrsiebeck.com/en
Email: info@mohrsiebeck.com
Address: Postfach 2040, D-72010 Tübingen, Germany
Submission Guidelines: https://www.mohrsiebeck.com/en/service
/for-authors

MOODY PUBLISHERS

Overview: Moody is a nonprofit Christian publisher that was founded
by D. L. Moody in 1894. It publishes Bible commentaries, books related to spiritual growth and renewal, and fiction. Sales from the
books are donated to The Moody Bible Institute.
Website: https://www.moodypublishers.com
Email: mpcustomerservice@moody.edu

Address: 820 North LaSalle Boulevard, Chicago, IL 60610
Submission Guidelines: https://www.moodypublishers.com/About
/faq/submitting-proposals

OXFORD UNIVERSITY PRESS (OUP)

Overview: Oxford Academic is the research and academic arm of OUP, the world's largest university press. It publishes scholarship and research in the arts and humanities, law, medicine and health, science and mathematics, and social sciences.
Website: https://global.oup.com
Email: custserv.us@oup.com
Address: Great Clarendon Street, Oxford, OX2 6DP, United Kingdom
Submission Guidelines: https://academic.oup.com/pages/authoring
/books/submitting-a-proposal

PAULIST PRESS

Overview: The Paulist Press is a Roman Catholic publisher founded in 1858 by the Paulist Fathers, a society of missionary priests. They publish books from different Christian traditions and even of other religions. Their catalog consists of academic books, professional or clergy books, popular books, and children's books. They accept un-solicited manuscripts.
Website: https://www.paulistpress.com
Email: submissions@paulistpress.com
Address: 997 Macarthur Boulevard, Mahwah, NJ 07430-9990
Submission Guidelines: https://www.paulistpress.com/Pages/Center
/auth_res_0.aspx

PETER LANG

Overview: Peter Lang is an academic publisher that focuses on quality work in the humanities and social sciences, specializing in cultural studies, education, film studies, history, law, linguistics and trans-lation, literature, media and communication, and philosophy and

theology. It has a worldwide readership, and its publications are often reviewed in international academic journals. It welcomes monograph proposals, including dissertations.
Website: https://www.peterlang.com
Email: publishing@peterlang.com
Address: 80 Broad Street, Fl 5, New York, NY 10004-4145
Submission Guidelines: https://www.peterlang.com/for-authors /#tiles-v2/policies-downloads

PICKWICK PUBLICATIONS

Overview: Pickwick Publications is the scholarly imprint of Wipf and Stock. It publishes books written for and by the academy, specializing in monographs, dissertations, and collections of conference papers in the fields of religion, philosophy, and related disciplines.
Website: https://wipfandstock.com/search-results/?imprint=pickwick-publications
Email: proposal@wipfandstock.com.
Address: 199 West 8th Avenue, Suite 3, Eugene, OR 97401-2960
Submission Guidelines: https://wipfandstock.com/submitting-a-proposal

PRESBYTERIAN & REFORMED PUBLISHING (P&R)

Overview: P&R was founded in 1930 and publishes books that promote biblical understanding and godly living as summarized in the Westminster Confession of Faith and Catechisms. Its titles span from academic works on the Bible and theology to popular books for lay readers. Such works include topics such as apologetics and evangelism, Bible study, biblical reference, Christian living, church ministry, counseling, Reformed traditions, theology, women's resources, worldviews, and ethics. It also publishes fiction and works for young people.
Website: https://www.prpbooks.com
Email: acquisitions@prpbooks.com
Address: 1102 Marble Hill Road, Phillipsburg, NJ 08865
Submission Guidelines: https://www.prpbooks.com/manuscript-submissions

REFORMATION HERITAGE BOOKS (RHB)

Overview: RHB is a confessionally Reformed publisher whose mission is to convert unbelievers and equip believers to serve Christ and his church through biblical, experiential, and practical ministry. Its works seek to be consistent with the historic Reformed creeds—namely, the Three Forms of Unity (the Belgic Confession, the Heidelberg Catechism, and the Canons of Dort) and the Westminster Standards.
Website: https://www.heritagebooks.org
Email: orders@heritagebooks.org
Address: 3070 29th Street SE, Grand Rapids, MI 49512
Submission Guidelines: Call 616-226-4884

SMYTH & HELWYS BOOKS

Overview: Smyth & Helwys was established in 1991 and is named after two pioneers of religious liberty, John Smyth (1554–1612) and Thomas Helwys (1550–1616). It offers a wide range of books including Christian living (devotional and inspirational material), ministry and leadership, and biblical studies (commentaries, Old and New Testament studies).
Website: https://www.helwys.com
Email: proposals@helwys.com
Address: 6316 Peake Road, Macon, GA 31210-3960
Submission Guidelines: https://www.helwys.com/submit-a-man uscript

THOMAS NELSON

Overview: Thomas Nelson was founded in Scotland in 1798. Today, it is a subsidiary of HarperCollins. Its mission is to inspire "the world by meeting the needs of people with content that promotes biblical principles and honors Jesus Christ. It is a world-leading publisher and provider of Christian content." This publisher does not accept unsolicited manuscripts but requires that you work through a professional literary agent.

Website: www.thomasnelson.com
Address: PO Box 141000, Nashville, TN 37214
Submission Guidelines: https://www.thomasnelson.com/about-us /manuscript-submission

TYNDALE HOUSE PUBLISHERS

Overview: Tyndale House was founded in 1962 by Dr. Kenneth Taylor as a venue for publishing the Living Bible. Today, Tyndale publishes Christian fiction, nonfiction, children's books, and other resources (including the New Living Translation). Tyndale does not accept unsolicited manuscripts but only those submitted by a professional literary agent.
Website: www.tyndale.com
Address: 351 Executive Drive, Carol Stream, IL 60188
Submission Guidelines: https://www.tyndale.com/faq

WESTMINSTER JOHN KNOX PRESS (WJK)

Overview: WJK is part of the Presbyterian Publishing Corporation, the publishing division of the Presbyterian Church USA. This company is the result of a 1988 merger of Westminster Press and John Knox Press. It publishes works for the academy and for the church in the areas of theology, biblical studies, preaching, worship, ethics, and religion and culture.
Website: https://www.wjkbooks.com
Email: submissions@wjkbooks.com
Address: 100 Witherspoon Street, Louisville, KY 40202-1396
Submission Guidelines: https://www.wjkbooks.com/Pages/Item /1345/Author-Relations.aspx

WIPF AND STOCK PUBLISHERS

Overview: Wipf and Stock is an independent publisher that produces quality books in biblical studies, classic theology, poetry, and history. It values solid academic research and accepts unsolicited manuscripts. Cascade Books and Pickwick Publications are its imprints.

Website: https://wipfandstock.com
Email: proposal@wipfandstock.com
Address: 199 West 8th Avenue, Suite 3, Eugene, OR 97401-2960
Submission Guidelines: https://wipfandstock.com/submitting-a-pro
posal

ZONDERVAN (ACADEMIC)

Overview: Founded in 1931, Zondervan is a subsidiary of Harper-
Collins and is one of the top Bible publishers in the world (it owns
the rights to the New International Version). It publishes titles on
spiritual growth, memoirs, apologetics, biographies, and church curricula. Zondervan Academic is the scholarly and academic imprint
and publishes college and seminary textbooks as well as ministry
resources.
Website: https://www.zondervan.com
Email: submissions@zondervan.com
Address: 3900 Sparks Drive SE, Grand Rapids, MI 49546
Submission Guidelines: https://www.zondervan.com/about-us/man
uscript-submissions

Academic Journals

Biblica

Biblica is a peer-reviewed research journal published quarterly by the Pontifical Biblical Institute, which is an institution in Rome run by the Jesuits. Articles in this journal concern the Old and New Testaments along with intertestamental literature and deal with various fields of research such as exegesis, philology, and history. Contributors come from a variety of backgrounds, and articles may be published in English, French, German, Italian, and Spanish.

Biblical Interpretation

Biblical Interpretation is a peer-reviewed academic journal published by Brill. Five issues are released each year, some simultaneously. This journal publishes articles and reviews concerning various aspects of critical biblical scholarship. Contributors come from a variety of theological and social backgrounds, though mainly from Western countries.

Bibliotheca Sacra

Bibliotheca Sacra is a theological journal published by Dallas Theological Seminary. Article and review topics range the spectrum of theological and biblical studies including biblical ministry. Contributors are largely from a conservative, evangelical background with a dispensational slant, and the articles reflect that viewpoint.

Bulletin for Biblical Research

Bulletin for Biblical Research is the journal of the Institute for Biblical Research (an organization of evangelical Christian scholars with specialties in the Old and New Testaments) and is published quarterly by Penn State University Press. This peer-reviewed journal focuses on Old Testament (Hebrew Bible) and New Testament studies and sometimes publishes cognate literature from various historical and literary approaches. A large portion of each issue is dedicated to current reviews of new publications on these subjects.

Catholic Biblical Quarterly

Catholic Biblical Quarterly is a refereed theological journal that is published quarterly by the Catholic Biblical Association of America. This journal publishes highly academic biblical and theological articles, and each issue includes an extensive section of book reviews.

Criswell Theological Review

Criswell Theological Review is a biannual academic journal from Criswell College. Topics range widely on various contemporary issues in biblical and theological studies. This journal also includes numerous book reviews. Contributors are mainly from conservative evangelical backgrounds with a Baptist slant, though some articles may diverge from those positions.

Detroit Baptist Seminary Journal

The *Detroit Baptist Seminary Journal* is an annual academic journal that is released every July by the Detroit Baptist Theological Seminary. This journal covers an array of contemporary theological, exegetical, and ministerial issues. The articles are written from a conservative, evangelical point of view.

Early Christianity

This journal is published quarterly by Mohr Siebeck in Germany. The journal is concerned with early Christianity as a historical phenomenon and aims to overcome certain limitations that have hindered the development of the discipline, including the concept of the "New Testament" itself. The journal covers not only the first Christian century but also the second. It also strives to reflect a multiplicity of contexts from a variety of perspectives.

Evangelical Quarterly

Evangelical Quarterly is an international, peer-reviewed journal published four times a year by Brill. Essays and book reviews span topics related to the Old and New Testaments, biblical and systematic theology, church history, pastoral theology, missions, and apologetics. Contributors come from a wide range of social and educational backgrounds but are expected to be reverent in their exposition of the evangelical Christian faith. This journal seeks to serve both the academy and the church.

Filología Neotestamentaria

Filología Neotestamentaria is published once a year in September by the Department of Greek Science Antiquity and the Middle Ages at the University of Córdoba in Madrid. Articles in this journal relate to New Testament textual criticism, grammar, semantics, lexicography, and semiotics (and their relationship with classical or Hellenistic Greek). Though Spanish is the main language, other languages such as French, English, German, and Italian are admitted.

Hebrew Bible and Ancient Israel

This is a peer-reviewed journal published quarterly by Mohr Siebeck in Germany. It focuses primarily on the biblical texts in their ancient historical contexts, but also on the history of Israel, with each issue having a topical focus. Although the primary language is English, essays in German and French are also admitted. The aim of the journal is "to foster discussion among different academic cultures within a larger international context pertaining to the study of the Hebrew Bible and ancient Israel in the first millennium BCE."

Horizons in Biblical Theology

This peer-reviewed journal is published twice a year by Brill. It addresses various aspects of the relationship between biblical studies and theology, including "traditional historical readings of biblical texts, thematic studies within biblical texts and theology, explorations of methodology and hermeneutics, and even readings from within confessional traditions."

Interpretation: A Journal of Bible and Theology

This journal is published by Union Presbyterian Seminary in Virginia. It offers "pastors, scholars, and theologians a valuable resource for study, preaching, and teaching." Each issue is themed, containing four to five major essays, along with book reviews.

Journal for the Study of Judaism in the Persian, Hellenistic, and Roman Period

This is a quarterly journal published by Brill. It "is a leading international forum for scholarly discussions on the history, literature and religious ideas on Judaism in the Persian, Hellenistic, and Roman period. It provides biblical scholars, students of rabbinic literature, classicists, and historians with essential information." This journal also includes a lengthy book review section.

Journal for the Study of the Historical Jesus

This journal is published by Brill and consists of three issues per year. It "provides an international forum for the academic discussion of Jesus within his first-century context. . . . The journal investigates the social, cultural, and historical context in which Jesus lived, discusses methodological issues surrounding the reconstruction of the historical Jesus, examines the history of research on Jesus and explores how the life of Jesus has been portrayed in historiographical reception and other media. The *Journal for the Study of the Historical Jesus* presents articles and book reviews discussing the latest developments in academic research in order to shed new light on Jesus and his world."

Journal for the Study of the New Testament

The *Journal for the Study of the New Testament* is issued five times a year by Sage Publications. This is a peer-reviewed, cutting-edge academic journal that focuses on all aspects in the field of New Testament studies and with essays written for scholars and advanced students. Contributors come from a variety of theological perspectives.

Journal for the Study of the Old Testament

This journal is published by Sage Publications, which releases five issues a year. It "has become widely regarded as offering the best in current scholarship on the Old Testament across a range of critical methodologies. Many original and creative approaches to the interpretation of the Old Testament literature and cognate fields of inquiry are pioneered in this journal, which showcases the work of both new and established scholars."

Journal of Biblical Literature

The *Journal of Biblical Literature* is published quarterly by the Society of Biblical Literature. It aims to promote critical and academic biblical scholarship. The content of this journal includes scholarly articles related to the "canon, cognate literature, and the historical matrix of the Bible," along with book reviews.

Journal of Early Christian Studies

This is a quarterly journal that is published by Johns Hopkins University Press. It "focuses on the study of Christianity in the context of late ancient societies and religions from 100–700 CE. The Journal publishes the best of traditional patristics scholarship while showcasing articles that call attention to newer methodologies and themes often absent from other patristic journals. Every issue features an extensive book review section. *Journal of Early Christian Studies* is the official publication of the North American Patristics Society (NAPS)."

Journal of Near Eastern Studies

This journal is published twice a year by the University of Chicago Press. It publishes on various aspects of the civilizations of the Near East, from the ancient times to premodern, including essays related to Assyriology, Egyptology, Hittitology, and the Hebrew Bible. The disciplinary range of the journal includes history, language, religion, literature, and archaeology. A substantial book review section is found in every issue.

Journal of the Evangelical Theological Society

The *Journal of the Evangelical Theological Society* is an academic peer-reviewed journal published quarterly by the Evangelical Theological Society. Articles cover research concerning theological disciplines that are centered in biblical literature. The doctrinal basis of this journal centers on an evangelical understanding of the inerrancy of Scripture and a trinitarian understanding of God. Contributors are expected to write in harmony with this doctrinal perspective.

Journal of Theological Interpretation

The *Journal of Theological Interpretation* is a peer-reviewed academic journal published twice a year by Penn State University Press. Articles include areas such as exegesis, theological method, history of interpretation, hermeneutical challenges, and reviews of major books. This journal emphasizes the concerns of the Theological Interpretation of Scripture movement. Contributors come from a variety of traditions and backgrounds.

Journal of Theological Studies

This journal is published by Oxford University Press twice a year. It "crosses the entire range of theological research, scholarship, and interpretation. Ancient and modern texts, inscriptions, and documents that have not before appeared in type are also reproduced."

New Testament Studies

New Testament Studies is an international peer-reviewed academic journal published quarterly by Cambridge University Press under the auspices of Studiorum Novi Testamenti Societas. This journal publishes articles in English, French, and German concerning a wide range of issues related to the "origins, history, context, and theology of the New Testament and early Christianity." Articles represent cutting-edge research from a variety of methods. "The periodical embraces exegetical, historical, literary-critical, sociological, theological and other approaches to the New Testament."

Novum Testamentum

Novum Testamentum is an international academic journal published quarterly by Brill. Articles are written in English, French, and German and cover topics related to the New Testament and early Christian texts, including text-critical, philological, and exegetical studies. Each volume also includes an extensive book review section.

Southeastern Theological Review

This is an academic journal published biannually (spring and fall) by Southeastern Baptist Theological Seminary. The fall issue is non-themed, and the spring issue is themed. Topics range from Bible to theology, history, ethics, philosophy, preaching, and counseling.

Southern Baptist Journal of Theology

The *Southern Baptist Journal of Theology* is an academic journal published three times a year (quarterly until 2018) by the Southern Baptist Theological Seminary. Each issue revolves around a particular theme (or book of the Bible). Contributors are largely from a Southern Baptist background and reflect its distinctives.

Trinity Journal

Trinity Journal is a peer-reviewed academic journal published twice a year by Trinity Evangelical Divinity School (TEDS). Topics cover a range of current biblical and theological issues. This journal is edited by the school's faculty, and the contributors are expected to write in harmony with the evangelical position of TEDS.

Tyndale Bulletin

The *Tyndale Bulletin* is a peer-reviewed academic journal published twice a year by Tyndale House in Cambridge. It publishes essays that make an original contribution to Old and New Testament studies. Contributors are expected to produce articles compatible with Tyndale House's doctrinal position, which is broadly evangelical and conservative.

Westminster Theological Journal

The *Westminster Theological Journal* is an academic journal published twice a year from Westminster Theological Seminary. Essays relate to theology, church history, ethics, and biblical interpretation. Each issue also includes numerous book reviews. The journal is edited by the faculty of Westminster, and contributors are expected to write from a conservative, evangelical, and Reformed viewpoint.

APPENDIX C

Religious Academic Organizations

Adventist Theological Society (ATS)

American Society of Church History (ASCH)

European Association of Biblical Studies (EABS)

Evangelical Missiological Society (EMS)

Evangelical Philosophical Society (EPS)

Evangelical Theological Society (ETS)

Institute for Biblical Research (IBR)

International Organization for Masoretic Studies (IOMS)

International Organization for Qumran Studies (IOQS)

International Organization for Septuagint and Cognate Studies (IOSCS)

International Organization for Targumic Studies (IOTS)

International Organization for the Study of the Old Testament (IOSOT)

International Syriac Language Project (ISLP)

Near Eastern Archaeological Society (NEAS)

Society for New Testament Studies (SNTS)

Society for Old Testament Study (SOTS)

Society of Biblical Literature (SBL)

Society of Christian Philosophers (SCP)

Annotated Bibliography

Adler, Mortimer J., and Charles Van Doren. *How to Read a Book: The Classic Guide to Intelligent Reading.* New York: Touchstone, 1972. Although this book is several decades old, the content continues to help readers comprehend material. The authors guide readers through four levels of reading (elementary, inspectional, analytical, and synoptic) and continue with chapters instructing readers how to read various kinds of writing from literature to history to philosophy and the sciences. The book concludes with discussions that prompt readers to consider their own goals for reading and the effects of reading on the mind of the individual.

Boice, Robert. *Professors as Writers: A Self-Help Guide to Productive Writing.* 4th edition. Stillwater, OK: New Forums, 1990. Boice describes his book as a self-help manual for academics with busy course loads and pressures to publish. He begins with an examination of the problems writers face and offers strategies and a regimen for productivity.

Booth, Wayne, et al. *The Craft of Research.* 4th edition. Chicago: University of Chicago Press, 2016. This book takes writers from research to writing with detailed directions for moving from the research question to the research problem, and then to crafting an argument. It includes helpful details concerning academic writing, such as how to incorporate sources, organize your argument, draft, and revise. Writing introductions and conclusions can be challenging, so the chapter on those is a useful resource for any writer's tool chest.

Brande, Dorothea. *Becoming a Writer*. New York: Tarcher/Putnam, 1934. Although this book was first published in the 1930s and is geared toward fiction writers, Brande's discussion of the difficulties writers in general face helps writers overcome these roadblocks and write, as does her advice concerning writing schedules. She also includes insightful discussions on critiquing your own work and on taking advice from others.

Challies, Tim. *Do More Better: A Practical Guide to Productivity*. Minneapolis: Cruciform, 2015. While this text is not specifically a book about writing, it is helpful for writers because it aims to move individuals to productivity. It guides readers to set achievable goals, plan their calendars, and consistently work at their tasks. There is a bonus chapter on taming email, the great thief of writing time.

Clark, Roy Peter. *Writing Tools: 55 Essential Strategies for Every Writer*. New York: Little, Brown, 2016. Arguably, the best things about this book are all the bits of instructional information. Clark implores readers to put action in verbs, not adverbs, and he teaches writers the importance of varying sentence and paragraph length. He does it all with examples from published texts. Additionally, he encourages writers to build habits that lead to success.

Currey, Mason. *Daily Rituals: How Artists Work*. New York: Knopf, 2013. This book is a survey of how over 150 artists—musicians, scientists, philosophers, politicians, and writers—work. In sum, it demonstrates that art is work, and successful artists work at their art.

Donovan, Melissa. *10 Core Practices for Better Writing*. San Francisco: Swan Hatch, 2013. Donovan explains that "this book is for people who are ready to commit to producing better writing" (page 2). She encourages her readers to develop productive habits in reading, writing, revision, grammar, skills, and processing feedback. She also discusses tools and resources; creativity and inspiration; and community, industry, and audience. So many habits can be overwhelming, so she instructs her readers to incorporate just one new habit each month.

Fau, Mauricio. *How to Write a Monograph*. Self-published, 2021. Many academic institutions expect professors to publish a monograph to be considered for tenure or promotion, but there are few instructional texts that address this task. Fau has published this short guide to walk writers through this process from choosing their topic to penning their concluding paragraph. He also provides a useful discussion of the differences between explanations and arguments.

Goins, Jeff. *You Are a Writer: So Start Acting like One.* Columbia, SC: Tribe, 2012. Goins divides the advice in this book into three sections: writing, getting read, and taking action. He acknowledges the challenges writers face and implores writers to establish their own platform and network as much as possible.

Goldberg, Natalie. *Wild Mind: Living the Writer's Life.* New York: Bantam, 1990. In sixty-two short chapters, Goldberg gets her readers writing. She shares her own successes, failures, and habits. Some of the most helpful elements of this book are the "try this" sections, which present the reader with a writing-workshop-style task. These tasks will get readers thinking and writing.

———. *Writing Down the Bones: Freeing the Writer Within.* Boston: Shambhala, 2005. This book is a humorous peek into Goldberg's writing workshops. As in *Wild Mind*, she shares personal writing anecdotes as she encourages her readers to write.

Goodson, Patricia. *Becoming an Academic Writer: 50 Exercises for Paced, Productive, and Powerful Writing.* 2nd edition. Thousand Oaks, CA: Sage, 2017. Goodson's belief that people become writers through practice is the crux of this book. She begins with a section preparing writers to practice by building a writing habit and increasing vocabulary and grammar knowledge. The second half of the book is filled with various exercises to get her readers writing.

Gupta, Nijay K. *The Writer: A Guide to Research, Writing, and Publishing in Biblical Studies.* Eugene, OR: Cascade Books, 2022. Gupta guides readers through the process of writing, from choosing a topic to researching, to drafting, to publishing. He also offers advice on note-taking and best practices for writing.

Harris, Robert. *Writing with Clarity and Style: A Guide to Rhetorical Devices for Contemporary Writers.* 2nd edition. New York: Routledge, 2017. Harris aims to help readers improve their writing style. Each of his sixteen chapters includes topics on style as well as review and discussion questions to help readers think through the topics addressed. The chapters also have sections that direct readers to the web for more information on the various topics. Many readers will find the appendices on blogging, business emails, and graduate school application essays beneficial.

Huff, Anne Sigismund. *Writing for Scholarly Publication.* Thousand Oaks, CA: Sage, 1999. Huff begins with audience. In order to publish, a writer must understand that scholarly writing is entering into and contributing to a larger academic conversation. She goes on to discuss the elements of a scholarly work such as the title, outline, introduction, and conclusion.

Jensen, Joli. *Write No Matter What: Advice for Academics.* Chicago: University of Chicago Press, 2017. This text specifically addresses the challenges to writing that academics face. How does a professor find the time or energy to write? How does an academic overcome nine of the most popular academic writing myths in order to write? Jensen addresses these questions in detail while encouraging scholars to keep their writing momentum going and build a writing support network.

Kibbe, Michael. *From Topic to Thesis: A Guide to Theological Research.* Downers Grove, IL: InterVarsity, 2016. In this short book, Kibbe helps theology students select a research topic, research the issues, and enter the scholarly conversation. The six appendices offer information concerning research databases as well as tips and timelines for writing.

King, Stephen. *On Writing: A Memoir of the Craft.* New York: Scribner, 2000. Because he is one of the most prolific and successful contemporary authors, writers of all genres—including academic writers—will benefit from the literary insights and tips King offers in this memoir. Readers will also come to understand that writing does not just happen. King works at it—regularly and consistently.

Lamott, Anne. *Bird by Bird: Some Instructions on Writing and Life.* 2nd edition. New York: Anchor, 2019. Lamott's text resembles a writing workshop, offering humorous encouragement to anyone who wants to write. Although this book is geared toward fiction writers, her directives to get started, find readers to give you critical feedback on your work, and find your voice will prove useful to many budding writers.

LaRocque, Paula. *The Book on Writing: The Ultimate Guide to Writing Well.* Arlington, TX: Grey & Guvnor, 2003. LaRocque boils down what she has learned over her thirty-year writing and teaching career into 238 pages packed with tips and advice to improve her readers' writing. The first section is all about the mechanics of writing. She teaches readers how to say what they mean concisely and appropriately. The second section focuses on storytelling devices that prove helpful for academic essays and monographs as well. The last section is a handbook of information where readers can read about comma usage as well as word-choice issues, such as "everyday" versus "every day."

Le Peau, Andrew T. *Write Better: A Lifelong Editor on Craft, Art, and Spirituality.* Downers Grove, IL: InterVarsity, 2019. Le Peau focuses his advice to nonfiction writers. As a writer and editor, he offers insights that are sympathetic and encouraging. He begins with the audience and spends two chapters discussing the art of persuasion. He goes on to provide tips on writing good prose and concludes with a section on the spirituality of writing, encouraging his readers to glorify God through their writing.

Miller-Cochran, Susan, Roy Stamper, and Stacey Cochran. *An Insider's Guide to Academic Writing: A Brief Rhetoric*. 3rd edition. Boston: Bedford/St. Martin's, 2022. This text is geared toward college students and begins by discussing what it means to write within academic disciplines. The authors help readers work through the writing process, and each chapter includes an example of a specific type of writing and a prompt for readers to write their own essay. The second half of the text explores writing within various academic disciplines such as the humanities, social sciences, natural sciences, and applied fields.

Murray, Rowena. *Writing for Academic Journals*. 4th edition. London: Open University Press, 2020. Murray begins by presenting thoughtful reasons for writing and publishing while acknowledging fears and anxieties that keep academics from writing. She goes on to help her readers target appropriate journals for their work, find the time to write, and work through the writing process from developing an argument to publishing and marketing.

Newport, Cal. *Deep Work: Rules for Focused Success in a Distracted World*. New York: Grand Central, 2016. Newport recognizes the deficit of deep work in today's society. He argues that deep work—focused attention to improve or master a skill and be productive—is valuable, rare, and meaningful. He goes on to explain how readers can move away from shallow work and into deep work. Although this book is not specifically about writing, the principles discussed may help writers focus on their work and increase their productivity.

O'Brien, Brandon J. *Writing for Life and Ministry: A Practical Guide to the Writing Process for Teachers and Preachers*. Chicago: Moody, 2020. O'Brien acknowledges the struggles he has as a preacher who desires to write, and he offers advice and exercises for his readers who want to write but don't feel like writers. He outlines the process of writing with additional exercises to move his readers to action. The chapters are short enough to digest easily, and his tone is consistently encouraging.

Perman, Matt. *How to Get Unstuck: Breaking Free from Barriers to Your Productivity*. Grand Rapids: Zondervan, 2018. Perman acknowledges that people often get stuck in their work and feel frustrated because they are not being productive. He writes this book to help his readers get unstuck in "a God-centered, gospel-driven way" (page 13). Getting unstuck includes knowing and understanding God's purposes for your work, managing your time well so that you can focus on your work, and overcoming obstacles that hinder your work.

Prior, Karen Swallow. *On Reading Well: Finding the Good Life through Great Books.* Grand Rapids: Brazos, 2018. Writing well hinges on reading well, and Prior strives to teach her readers how to do that. She explains that reading well is reading virtuously, closely, accurately, and insightfully, and she connects reading to the cardinal virtues, the theological virtues, and the heavenly virtues. For example, she uses *A Tale of Two Cities* to demonstrate how reading can reveal our own ideas of justice while simultaneously shaping this cardinal virtue in our minds.

Provost, Gary. *100 Ways to Improve Your Writing: Proven Professional Techniques for Writing with Style and Power.* Updated edition. New York: Berkley, 2019. This handbook for writing could be read from cover to cover or used as a reference tool. Provost dedicates the first nine chapters to improving your writing and the next nine to overcoming writer's block. He then launches into tips for writing a strong introduction and general tips on strengthening your writing. If you want to avoid splitting infinitives or understand when to use a colon, there are short chapters (one to two pages) that address these topics and a host of other style issues.

Rabiner, Susan, and Alfred Fortunato. *Thinking like Your Editor: How to Write Great Serious Nonfiction and Get It Published.* New York: Norton, 2002. As the title suggests, Rabiner and Fortunato urge their readers to think like an editor. That means think about your audience from the start. Shape your work to your audience. The authors walk readers through writing a proposal, compiling a submission package, and submitting a manuscript to a publisher. The second section of the book focuses on the specifics of writing nonfiction well, and the final section delves into marketing. A sample proposal is included in the appendix.

Rocco, Tonette S., and Tim Hatcher, eds. *The Handbook of Scholarly Writing and Publishing.* San Francisco: Jossey-Bass, 2011. This book is a four-part collection of essays on academic writing. The first section includes essays that encourage scholars to publish, even during their graduate studies. The second section offers essays for improving your writing by finding your voice and developing your research problem. The third and fourth sections focus on preparing your manuscript and reflecting on the process, respectively. Readers are encouraged to become reviewers as part of their journey to becoming published authors.

Strunk, William, Jr., and E. B. White. *The Elements of Style*. 4th edition. Boston: Pearson, 2000. This short little handbook is full of helpful guidelines for writers, from comma usage to consistent verb tense. A quick read-through of the eighty-five pages will help readers improve their writing style and make them mindful of ways to write clearly and concisely.

Sword, Helen. *Air & Light & Time & Space: How Successful Academics Write*. Cambridge, MA: Harvard University Press, 2017. In this book, Sword focuses on habits. She implores her readers to develop habits for productive writing. Find the time and place to write and make it part of the rhythm of your life. Work to improve your craft by writing for, with, and among other writers, and strive to make the process enjoyable.

———. *Stylish Academic Writing*. Cambridge, MA: Harvard University Press, 2012. Sword argues that most academic writing ignores the advice concerning style and grace that Strunk, White, Colomb, and others have offered for decades. She pleads with academics to incorporate a style equal to the substance of their work. With chapters on voice, hooks, structure, and creativity, Sword teaches academics to become stylish writers.

Turabian, Kate L. *A Manual for Writers of Research Papers, Theses, and Dissertations*. 9th edition. Chicago: University of Chicago Press, 2018. This text instructs readers how to write up their research, reference sources following *The Chicago Manual of Style*, and appropriately execute various elements of punctuation. Most publishers within the field of theological studies follow the Chicago style. Be sure to research the style guide used by your intended publisher and follow that guide from the beginning of your work.

Ueland, Brenda. *If You Want to Write*. Mansfield Centre, CT: Martino, 2011 (originally published 1938). Ueland frees her readers from their own insecurities and encourages them to write. She highlights the importance of imagination and champions the idea that everyone has something important to say.

Vyhmeister, Nancy Jean. *Your Guide to Writing Quality Research Papers: For Students of Religion and Theology*. Grand Rapids: Zondervan, 2014. Vyhmeister helps her readers understand what research is and what it is not. She discusses different kinds of research, including biblical, literary, and human subject research, and different kinds of writing, from research papers to dissertations and journal articles. The bulk of this text delves into the nuts and bolts of carrying out and presenting research.

Williams, Joseph M., and Joseph Bizup. *Style: Lessons in Clarity and Grace.* 13th edition. London: Pearson, 2020. This classic work is in its 12th print edition with an electronic 13th edition available. Williams and Bizup help readers understand style and take action to improve their own writing style. This text is similar to, but more detailed than, *Style: The Basics of Clarity and Grace.*

Williams, Joseph M., and Joseph Bizup. *Style: The Basics of Clarity and Grace.* 5th edition. London: Pearson, 2014. Not only do Williams and Bizup help readers improve their writing style, but they also help them understand exactly what style is. With chapters on actions, characters, concision, and elegance, this book guides readers to improve their writing. In fact, the inside cover includes "Ten Principles for Writing Clearly."

Zerubavel, Eviatar. *The Clockwork Muse: A Practical Guide to Writing Theses, Dissertations, and Books.* Cambridge, MA: Harvard University Press, 1999. Zerubavel argues that writing does not just happen. Instead, serious writers must adopt workable writing schedules to achieve their writing goals. He leads readers through the process of creating schedules and differentiating A-time from B-time in order to maximize productivity.

Zinsser, William. *On Writing Well: The Classic Guide to Writing Nonfiction.* 7th edition. Revised and updated. New York: Harper Perennial, 2006. Zinsser helps his readers understand that they must write in a way that will make other people want to read their work. Writers must write to an audience. He claims that this book is a complement to Strunk and White in that he applies their "principles to the various forms that nonfiction writing and journalism can take" (page x). He focuses on writing interviews, travel, memoirs, science, business, sports, criticism, and humor.

Index

157